The Passionate Gardener

The
Passionate
Gardener

Georgia Raimondi

THE READER'S DIGEST ASSOCIATION, INC.
Pleasantville, New York / Montreal

A Reader's Digest Book
Conceived and created by Georgia Raimondi

EDITOR	Melanie Hulse
ART DIRECTOR/DESIGNER	Larissa Lawrynenko
PRINCIPAL PHOTOGRAPHER	Eleanor Thompson
CONTRIBUTING PHOTOGRAPHER	Maggie Oster
ILLUSTRATION RENDERINGS	Jeremy Dawson
ILLUSTRATED BORDERS	Mick Ellison
PHOTO ASSISTANT	Darryl Arbesman
FOOD STYLIST	Roberta K. Rall
COPY EDITOR	Edward W. Atkinson
FOOD/CRAFTS CONSULTANT	Maryanne Bannon
GARDENING CONSULTANT	Ruth Rogers Clausen

IMPORTANT: Every effort has been made to present clear and accurate instructions, therefore the author and publishers can accept no liability for any injury, illness, or damage which may inadvertently be caused to the user while following these instructions. In the recipes, use either the American or metric measurements, not both. Exact conversions are not always possible. The essential oils used in the aromatherapy have very powerful properties. In this book, we explain some of them. For specific uses, it is vital that you consult your physician as well as a recognized aromatherapist.

The acknowledgments and credits that appear on pages 7 and 187 are hereby made a part of this copyright page.
Copyright © 1999 Georgia Raimondi
Photography copyright © 1999 Eleanor Thompson and Maggie Oster

Library of Congress Cataloging-in-Publication Data

Raimondi, Georgia.

    The passionate gardener / Georgia Raimondi.

    p. cm.

    Includes index.

    ISBN 0-7621-0074-5
    1.Gardening. 2. Holiday decorations. 3. Nature craft.
4. Cookery. 5. Seasons.   I. Title.
SB455.R27 1999
635—dc2l   98-4833

For my husband,
Michael Muffoletto, who is
always there for me

For my parents,
Sally and Buddy Raimondi,
a bouquet of love and gratitude
for encouraging me to
follow my dreams

"The only limit to
your garden is at the
boundaries of
your imagination."

—THOMAS D.
CHURCH

Acknowledgments

This book would not have been possible without the support of numerous friends and colleagues. I would like to extend my love and thanks especially to my sister, **Carolyn Wall**, *who has always been a rich source of inspiration and encouragement. Special and heartfelt thanks to* **Joseph Gonzalez**, *former executive editor of Reader's Digest Trade Books, and* **Henrietta Stern,** *senior design director, for taking a leap of faith with me. Sincere thanks to my art director,* **Larissa Lawrynenko**, *for working her magic to bring all the visual elements together so beautifully; to my editor,* **Melanie Hulse**, *for her thoughtful suggestions, ideas, and excellent editorial advice in making this a better book; and to the photographers,* **Eleanor Thompson**, *whose glowing photographs shine throughout the book, and* **Maggie Oster**, *for capturing the beauty of the garden. Thanks also to the talented staff at Reader's Digest Trade Books for their efforts in the production of this book; to my agents,* **Angela Miller** *and* **Coleen O'Shea**, *for their advice and enthusiasm; to* **Rona Bayer**, *a wonderful neighbor and friend, whose comments and careful reading of the manuscript were always helpful; to* **Bobbi Stuart** *for her dear friendship and helping hand in styling the holiday photos; to* **Kathy Delano** *for her fine eye and delicate touch in making the sachets. To my friends and family, especially* **Aunt Thelma** *and* **Uncle Chester**, *who supported and encouraged me at every stage of this labor of love—a huge thank you.*

CONTENTS

SUMMER 58

Autumn 100

WINTER 142

*"And forget not that
the earth delights to feel your
bare feet and the wind longs to
play with your hair."*
—KAHLIL GIBRAN

Introduction

REATING A GARDEN is an expression of the heart that harmonizes the spiritual, romantic, and poetic aspects of my nature. It enhances the quality of my life, inspires my creativity, and enriches my spirit. There is something both magical and mystical about growing things. When I plant a seed, I know it is an act of faith in things to come. This simple deed reminds me that a garden is a celebration of God's gracious and generous hand at work. The small miracle of tender green shoots poking through the rich brown soil is a satisfying fulfillment of that faith.

I have a working woman's garden. It's small enough that I can tend it without the help of a full-time gardener, but large enough to let me to feel that I am creating a place that is uniquely mine. It's a cozy, romantic, whimsical haven that suits the stone-and-slate English cottage it surrounds.

In many ways my garden tells the story of my life. Today, when I snip basil from plants just outside my kitchen door, the pungent aroma conjures up fond remembrances of my mother and aunt preparing pesto. With every new variety of tomato I try, I do so with thoughts of sharing the fruit with my father, a man whose love of tomatoes is unsurpassed. These rich scents are linked with reminiscences that have gently accumulated through the years and inspired my "someday, must-have" garden.

Gardens evolve over time. It takes patience and steady loving care to grow a garden that flourishes. My first garden was at a country home that my husband, Michael, and I had in Old Lyme, Connecticut. This was not a garden that flourished. Our rocky New England soil proved a real challenge. Also I was a weekend gardener who soon discovered that many cherished plants would bloom during the week then drop their spent petals on the ground, a disappointing greeting for me on Saturday morning.

I persevered and my passion for gardening began to be rewarded when we purchased an English Cotswold home—complete with a charming carriage house—in Fairfield County, Connecticut. With a sense of adventure, strong knees, and sturdy backs, Michael and I set about transform-

ing our staid suburban landscape into an exuberant mix of annual and perennial flowers, fragrant herbs, tall grasses, and lush shrubs. Freshly picked heirloom vegetables became staple foods for our table.

Notwithstanding the delectable appeal of the end result, it is the always-unfolding process of creating and maintaining a vibrant garden that I find most enjoyable. And because I try always to work with nature, my garden is constantly evolving and changing. To me a natural and unstudied look is inviting. I mix the ornamental with the edible, line paths with fragrant herbs, let roses tumble freely over arbors, and encourage myriad creatures to share in the joyful labor.

Gardening connects me to the natural world in many wonderful ways. I don't need to travel to a distant or exotic clime to feel part of the world's ecosystem. Observing the furred and feathered beings that inhabit my local landscape makes me keenly aware of my surroundings and encourages me to live in greater harmony with nature's laws. There is a special reward in

creating a welcoming garden habitat where butterflies glide on their dazzling wings, where songbirds nest and rear their hatchlings, where squirrels entertain with their daring acrobatic antics. Sharing a garden with wildlife gladdens my heart while enlivening the landscape with a rich tapestry of brilliant colors, melodious sounds, and graceful motion.

Whether you garden on a balcony, in a backyard, or on burgeoning acres, the splendor of the garden restores the soul. It is a place of inspiration and tranquillity where we can savor the wonders of nature. *The Passionate Gardener* celebrates all 12 months of the year and offers practical gardening information for each of them. Here you'll find easy-to-prepare recipes that call for fresh seasonal ingredients, as well as clear instructions for stylish decorating projects and delightful aromatherapy preparations that bring the bounty of the garden into the home. So come with me on this journey through the seasons and share the glory of nature. Although our climates may be different, the ideas presented in *The Passionate Gardener* are easily adapted to different gardening cycles and to your own busy lifestyle. My wish is that this book will prove to be a helpful companion and a joyful inspiration for getting the most from your garden and sharing its gifts with your friends, family, and neighbors.

Spring

"Spring had come once more... in a succession of sweet, fresh, chilly days, with pink sunsets, and miracles of resurrection and growth."

—L.M. MONTGOMERY

SPRING SONG

**S**PRING IS AN ever-renewing gift. It is a time of new beginnings, when every swelling bud, just-stirring sprout, and unfurling leaf is a true miracle in the making. As the days begin to lengthen, my spirits soar in anticipation of the dawn of this new season. Even before the ground starts to thaw, I'm eager to sink my hands into the dirt and I pace the garden, lifting and poking through the winter mulch, searching for the first tender shoots that signal the earth's reawakening.

With the passage of time, the sun climbs higher in the brilliant blue sky, the days grow milder, and the garden ends its hibernation with a boisterous burst of blooming—vivid yellow winter aconites, heavenly blue squills, crocuses and windflowers in a rainbow of pastel and vibrant colors, and *Iris reticulata* in their regal cloaks of blue and purple. Sprays of golden forsythia enliven the landscape while stately pussy willows, with velvety buds soft as cats' paws, grow plump, and dainty violets spring up all across the lawn.

Spring's noon is trumpeted by the arrival of creamy jonquils and sunny daffodils accompanied by the rich tones of blue-violet hyacinths. In the background, warm peach tulips sway above a carpet of sky blue forget-me-nots. Enticed by all this splendor, birds begin to make appearances, brightening the garden with flashing feathers and exuberant songs. A warbling wren guides his mate to their new nest and a robin splashes unabashedly in the birdbath. Bumblebees quiver among the branches of the apple tree, tippling nectar from the frothy blossoms.

The delicacies of the kitchen garden that begin to appear in late spring are irresistible. A garden-grown salad of young radishes, leafy greens, slim asparagus stalks, and tender peas is the perfect reward for a long day's labor. But even as a shadow of twilight sets in, I am reluctant to leave the outdoors. This grand spectacle of nature's quickening inspires me with childlike wonder and the longing to linger. But I put my tools away happily, confident of the eternal promise of the season, and knowing that spring's twilight is summer's dawn in the ever-renewing cycle of the seasons.

*"No matter what the almanac may say,
the year begins with the first month of spring,
when the snowdrifts into rivulets slip away,
and bluebirds of the coming violet sing."*

—LUCY LARCOM

A Spring Outing

Each spring I make my first trip to
the nursery with a carefully prepared
list and the cool determination that this
year I will resist all temptations and
buy only what is on my list.

At the nursery, I choose a sensibly
small wagon and join the eager crowd
waiting for the gates to open. But when
they finally open I have forgotten it all.
That meager list in my back pocket?
Forgotten. The promise I made to not let
my eyes be bigger than our garden?
Rapidly dissolving in the perfume of a
Gallica rose. I have become a wide-
eyed child in a botanical toy store wishing for at least one of everything.

My little wagon is chock full when I spot
those perky daisies that look like butterflies. I know I really shouldn't, but
who could resist? Certainly not me. After
all, I tell myself, spring comes only
once a year.

THINGS TO DO

Early

🌿 Prune trees, shrubs, and grapevines. Prune roses before new growth begins. Cut ornamental grasses to the ground. Remove fallen branches, twigs, and other debris from yard. Begin to remove winter mulch.

🌿 Test soil for pH and nutrient content, testing kits are available at home and garden centers. An agricultural school or government agency may test soil samples for a nominal fee.

🌿 Begin planting. Sow seeds of hardy vegetables such as radishes, lettuces, spinach and kale in a protected area of the garden or in a cold frame. Set out onion sets and plants for broccoli, cabbage, and Brussels sprouts as soon as they are available. Plant bareroot perennials.

Middle

🌿 Start seeds for tender vegetables and warm-season flowers indoors. Start caladiums, tuberous begonias, and similar plants indoors.

🌿 Sow hardy annuals, such as cosmos, larkspur, poppies, and cornflowers, outdoors.

"I think that if ever a mortal heard the voice of God it would be in a garden at the cool of the day."
—A. FRANFORT MOORE

Remove remainder of winter mulch from planting beds. Prepare beds by turning soil over and adding dehydrated cow manure and compost.

Plant bush fruits, strawberries, and new perennials.

Plant trees and shrubs, both evergreen and deciduous, including fruit trees. Transplant evergreen shrubs and trees. Soak bareroot roses before planting.

Prune early-flowering shrubs as soon as they finish blooming.

Fertilize perennials when new growth appears. Fertilize acid-loving shrubs and evergreens with 4-6-4 formula.

Divide crowded summer- or fall-blooming perennials. Divide snowdrops after flowers fade.

Late

Mulch as soon as the soil warms up.

When all danger of frost has passed, plant caladiums and tuberous begonias in a shady area. When night temperature remains at about 55°F (13°C), plant tender vegetables and annuals outdoors. Continue to plant perennials and roses. Plant summer-flowering bulbs and new chrysanthemums.

Sow seeds of biennials, such as hollyhocks and foxgloves, for flowering the following year. Keep the seed beds moist to ensure germination.

Mark areas for new fall bulb plantings with colored golf tees.

Ongoing

Deadhead flowers from spring bulbs; let foliage die back on its own.

Tie and train climbers.

Weed after rainstorms, being sure to remove weed's roots.

Clean and set out garden furniture.

Fire-up the grill and enjoy your first cook-out of the season.

THE GARDEN HABITAT

AS MORE AND more of our natural landscape diminishes in favor of increased development, birds, butterflies, and all the rest of our indigenous wildlife are being pushed into smaller and smaller areas and denied their normal sources of water, food, and shelter. We can improve the present and help to ensure the future for these wonderful creatures by turning our yards and gardens into supportive mini-habitats.

After we settled into our home, my husband Michael and I began reducing the size our large, high-maintenance lawn. We installed several small island beds and filled them with an array of native and cultivated plants. Since we like having plants of varying heights, we added some smaller trees and shrubs to complement the towering trees already on the property, and a mix of grasses and groundcovers as well. I later learned that parks and arboretums call this technique "layering" and use it to create hospitably diverse neighborhoods for birds and other wildlife. Another favorite setting is an "edge" habitat: a transitional area where one type of habitat adjoins and blends into another. Such areas offer another combination of food and shelter for birds, animals, and insects.

To create a welcoming habitat of your own, mix deciduous and evergreen trees and shrubs to ensure diverse shelter, camouflage, and food. Fruit trees, nut trees, and berry bushes will supply abundant food for chipmunks and squirrels, finches and waxwings, rabbits and raccoons. Evergreens such as white pine, juniper, and holly offer berries and seeds as well as safety from predators and refuge from foul weather. Food and shelter need not come from living plants. A layer of leaf mulch becomes a camouflage for the cocoons of pupating luna moths. So go a little wild; the rewards are many. Not only will you spend less time and money on maintenance, you will enjoy a garden that honors our covenant with the natural world.

"Blessed of the Lord be his land, for the precious things of heaven, for the dew, and for the deep that croucheth beneath, and for the precious fruits brought forth by the sun."

—DEUTERONOMY 33:13

March

Planting Tips

- Select plump, firm corms.
- Plant in early fall about 3 inches (8cm) deep.
- Good drainage is essential.
- Select soil that is light, sandy, and slightly alkaline.
- Full sun or light shade.
- Plant in groups of two dozen or more in one place.
- Apply bulb fertilizer as flowers fade.
- Do not cut back foliage, let it die back naturally.
- Crocus will form large colonies, spreading by producing new corms or reseeding.
- Divide crocuses when they are overcrowded, either in early fall or when leaves turn yellow in late spring or early summer.

THE CROCUS

SPRING, the vernal equinox, always arrives earlier than March 21 for me. This glorious, long-awaited season really begins with my first glimpse of the first crocus. Like all gardeners, I treasure the early signs of spring. And the crocus, more than any other flower that graces the garden, seems to lead us gently out of the darkness of winter into the light of spring.

The morning weather report may forecast another wintry day of frosty temperatures, blustery skies, and possible snow flurries, but my thoughts are filled with images of a warm, sun-drenched day spent planting in my garden. In my mind, my mittens and wool cap are happily exchanged for gardening gloves and a straw hat. This enchanting reverie is instantly conjured up by the sight of crocuses magically popping up all over the barren lawn like freshly dipped Easter eggs. What crocuses lack in size, they make up in numbers, covering the brown earth with a welcome profusion of springtime color.

Among the earliest sentries of the season, the snow crocus (*Crocus chrysanthus)*, announces the dawn of spring even before the last snow has melted. Although this wild species is smaller than its cousin, the common Dutch hybrid *(C. vernus)*, it rewards us by producing as many as 10 blooms from a single corm.

The delightful color blends and combinations of 'Blue Pearl,' 'Cream Beauty,' and 'Snow Bunting' bring splashes of color to my garden when little else is in bloom. I plant these sweet flowers where they are most likely to be visible and enjoyed—in raised beds, troughs, tubs, nestled between stones in my rock garden, or front-and-center at the edge of a flower border.

Gazing at a vibrant medley of crocuses in a painter's palette of gay shades of purple, mauve, violet, blue, orange, and yellow, I marvel at the ability such a small jewel of nature has to bring the spirit-lifting promise of longer, milder days to come.

"He who sees things grow from the beginning will have the best view of them."
—ARISTOTLE

FLOWERING BRANCHES

HIS IS THE time of year when my spirit yearns for green sprouts and signs of warmer weather to come. I like to hurry nature along with a glorious indoor display of blossoms from the cut branches of spring-flowering shrubs and trees. Forcing branches into bloom is not difficult, and a thoughtful selection of plants will ensure a succession of blooms for several months.

In order to bloom, the plants must have been dormant for 40 to 60 days in temperatures below 40°F (4°C), so choose branches that set their buds in fall or early winter (see Plant List at right). Look for branches with fat flower buds (the small buds are leaf buds). To preserve the shape and health of the plant, cut branches that you would normally prune.

Scrape about 2 inches (5cm) of bark from the cut end of the branch and make a 3- to 5-inch (8- to 10-cm) slit in the stem end to enhance water absorption. You can also split the end by hammering it gently; be careful to avoid crushing the branch, which would accelerate decay.

Fill a tall container with room-temperature water and place the cut branches in it. Or fill the bathtub and submerge the entire branch—buds and all. Let them soak overnight so that they will absorb as much water as possible. Fill a second container with cool water, add a floral preservative (available from florists), then transfer the branches to the new container. Place the branches in a cool, dimly lit place. In three or four days bring

Plant List

🍀 Blooming times and cutting times will vary according to your location and the weather conditions. In southern New England, the earliest bloomers are witch hazel (*Hamamelis mollis*), Cornelian cherry (*Cornus mas*), forsythia (*Forsythia* spp.), pussy willow (*Salix discolor*), azalea (*Rhododendron* spp.), and flowering quince (*Chaenomeles*).

🍀 For later forcing choose from magnolia, apple, and crab apple trees (*Malus* spp.), beach plum (*Prunus maritima*), flowering dogwood (*Cornus florida*), hawthorn (*Crataegus* spp.), red bud (*Cercis canadensis*), and mock orange (*Philadelphus* spp.).

branches into a bright area out of direct sunlight. Change the water and cut 1 inch (3cm) off the bottom of each stem every week. Mist the branches at least once a day. They may take as long as 3 weeks to bloom, but the sight of all those precious buds bursting with divine color is a glorious reward for your patient anticipation.

"In green underwood and cover Blossom by blossom Spring begins."
—A.C. SWINBURNE

Planting Tips

- Choose a container that is large enough to accommodate root growth.
- Ensure proper drainage. Punch or drill holes, use a liner pot, or fill the bottom with 1 inch (3cm) of gravel or pebbles.
- Make a rich planting medium by combining 2 parts sterile potting soil, 1 part perlite, and 1 part peat moss; include slow-release fertilizer at the rate recommended by the manufacturer.
- Combine plants that have similar needs for light and water.
- Put the first plant in the center then work your way to the outer edges. Use trailing plants in the front.
- Add a layer of mulch, such as cocoa bean hulls, on top to conserve soil moisture and to keep the soil surface looking neat.
- Containers dry out quickly. Check soil moisture often and water as needed.

CONTAINER GARDENING

 ONTAINERS ARE happily versatile and eminently mobile. Because they are portable, containers allow gardeners great flexibility. The soil's pH can be customized for plants not adapted to the garden and the plants themselves can be easily changed to suit the changing seasons or a special occasion. And the planters can be moved from site to site to fill in bare spots, to take the best advantage of sun and breezes, or simply to delight the gardener with color and fragrance.

Almost anything that grows in the ground can be grown in a pot—annuals, perennials, bulbs, tubers, corms, vegetables, herbs, vines, fruit, even small trees and shrubs. These plants and their containers can be used to enliven windowsills, stairways, entrances, terraces, porches, and decks, or to fill out flower beds and borders. Brimming with greens and edible flowers, my vintage wooden wagon is a movable feast. In the morning it sits by the front porch, but as the sun changes course, I simply pull the wagon up to the kitchen door where the nasturtiums, calendulas, violas, arugula, and mustard greens will reap the benefits of the afternoon sunshine and are handy for use in a dinnertime salad.

When it comes to selecting containers, I never limit myself to traditional flowerpots. With a little imagination—and some attention to providing drainage—almost anything can be made into a one-of-kind planter. The key is to match the plants to the personality of the container. A stone urn filled with feathery ferns and showy astilbe will brighten up a shady nook. A bare patch in the vegetable garden can be transformed with a lively display of dahlias, salvia, verbena, and trailing Swan River daisies—and mixing flowers and vegetables captures the effusive spirit of a cottage garden. There is almost no place that wouldn't be right for a pot and almost no plant that can't be potted—so let your creativity flourish.

"We can never have enough of nature. We must be refreshed by the sight of inexhaustible vigor."
—Henry David Thoreau

FLORAL KEEPSAKES

UCKED AMONG the pages of an old address book, I've secreted an abundance of exquisitely preserved garden gems. Whenever I open the book, pansies and violas come drifting out, their sweet floral faces greeting me with cheerful expressions. Turning the pages uncovers additional riches: rose petals in soft pastel hues and dainty old-fashioned flowers such as larkspur, verbena, columbines, coralbells, bleeding heart, forget-me-nots, and cosmos. All these inspire an array of special mementos designed to be cherished.

To create your own treasury of pressed flowers, choose flat, delicate flowers with thin petals such as pansies and Johnny-jump-ups, lacy leaves and fern fronds, slender grasses and fragrant herbs. For best results with plump or sculptured blossoms such as roses or larkspur, separate the petals and press them individually. Arrange

"There's rosemary, that's for remembrance, pray you, love, remember. And there is pansies, that's for thoughts."
—WILLIAM SHAKESPEARE

the chosen botanicals between the pages of an old telephone book or dictionary. (I like to sort them alphabetically, placing parsley, sage, and thyme between the pages of the P's, S's, and T's, tucking ferns among the F's, and scattering leaves of dusty miller, geranium, ivy, and lamb's ears throughout the D's, G's, I's and L's.) Then close the book and add gentle pressure by placing a weight, such as a brick, on top. Depending on the shape and thickness of the botanical, pressing and drying will take from 2 to 4 weeks.

Embellishing plain stationery or note cards with pressed flowers transforms a traditional gift into a celebration of individuality. An ordinary album decorated with thoughtfully selected and preserved blossoms becomes a priceless remembrance of a summer garden. Each gift of a handcrafted pressed botanical keepsake bestowed on a friend or loved one is a personal expression of caring and affection.

Materials

 Assorted pressed, dried botanicals, such as flowers or flower petals, herbs, ferns, leaves, or grasses

Assorted note cards, stationery, albums, bookmarks, place cards, gift cards, name tags, or picture frame mats

Rubber cement or white craft glue

Soft glue brush

Gold paint (optional)

Artist's brush (optional)

Tweezers

If desired, swirl gold paint onto the paper with an artist's brush before applying botanicals and let dry. Pressed, dried botanicals are brittle and fragile; handle them with care. To work out the design, use tweezers to position botanicals on the paper. When you are satisfied with the arrangement, carefully brush the underside of one botanical with glue and gently press it in position. Repeat with remaining elements, working one by one until the design is complete.

SPRING GREENS

LETTUCE WAS first cultivated more than 2,000 years ago in Egypt and it has been lauded by cooks and gardeners around the world ever since. A spring garden offers a rich repertoire of tempting greens—from the classic salad bowl varieties to gourmet delights such as peppery arugula, citrusy purslane, robust radicchio, nutty mache, sweet red oak leaf and buttery Bibb lettuce, piquant mustards, and pungent cresses. For a tempting contrast of tastes, mix sharp greens with sweet fruit such as pears, peaches, nectarines, or berries. Tender vegetables, like asparagus, peas, beans, and fennel also make tasty accompaniments. A fresh salad dressed with a tangy home-made dressing will enliven your springtime menu whether served as a first course, main course, or side dish.

Asparagus & Mesclun Salad
with Walnut-Mustard Dressing

Dressing: 1/2 cup (120ml) walnut oil

1/4 cup (60ml) white wine vinegar

1/2 tablespoon fresh lemon juice

1 tablespoon sugar

1 tablespoon Dijon mustard

1/4 teaspoon ground black pepper

2 tablespoons snipped green onion

In a blender or food processor combine the first six ingredients. Cover and process for about one minute. Add green onion and stir. Cover and refrigerate until needed. Yield: Approximately one cup (240ml)

Salad: 24 asparagus spears, blanched
(1 1/2 to 2 lbs; 3/4 to 1 kg, depending on size)

4 cups (115g) of mesclun greens

1/2 cup (63g) walnuts, chopped and toasted

To toast walnuts: Preheat oven to 350°F (177°C). Place nuts on a baking sheet, bake for about 15 minutes; stir and turn them occasionally until toasted evenly. Allow to cool. Divide greens onto 4 salad plates, top with asparagus. Drizzle dressing over salad. Garnish with toasted walnuts. Serves 4.

Pear, Arugula, Radicchio, & Gorgonzola Salad
with Raspberry Vinaigrette

Raspberry Vinaigrette: 1 cup (125g) fresh raspberries

1/4 cup (60ml) rice vinegar

1/2 cup (120ml) olive oil

1 tablespoon sugar

In a blender or food processor, purée raspberries and rice vinegar. Strain mixture to remove seeds. Discard seeds. Place mixture in a bowl, whisk in olive oil and sugar. Cover and refrigerate until needed. Yield: approximately one cup (240ml).

Salad: 1 bunch of arugula (washed and tough stems removed)

1 small head of radicchio (washed and leaves separated)

2 pears, cored and sliced

1/2 cup (60g) Gorgonzola, crumbled

Divide the greens onto 4 salad plates and place sliced pears on top. Drizzle dressing over pear slices and greens. Garnish with crumbled Gorgonzola cheese. Serves 4.

> "How sweetly smells
> the honeysuckle
> in the hushed night,
> as if the world were
> one of utter peace
> and love and
> gentleness."
> —WALTER SAVAGE
> LANFOR

FRAGRANT BATH BAGS

A LEISURELY BATH in a tub filled with steamy water infused with fragrant herbs and flowers is the perfect antidote for everyday stress and tension as well as overworked limbs and tired muscles.

Toss one of these sachets into the warm bath water to steep like a tea bag or tie one to the faucet so that the water runs over it while the bath is filling. The sachets can also be taken into the shower—gently rub one over your body and enjoy the full effect of the aromatic herbs. For gift-giving, make several bags, tie them with pretty ribbons, and arrange them in a decorative tin or small wicker basket.

Preparation

3 to 4 tablespoons per bag crushed dried herbs and flowers (single variety or a blend)

❧

Relaxing blend: calendula, chamomile, comfrey, elder flowers, lavender, jasmine, rose geranium leaves

Refreshing blend: lemon verbena, mint, rosemary, sage, thyme

❧

Cotton handkerchief or 8" x 8" square of cheese cloth, organdy, or muslin

String or colorfast ribbon

Make several bags at once—store the extras in a tin to retain freshness. Spoon the herbal mixture onto the handkerchief, pull up the corners, and tie them securely with string or colorfast ribbon. Discard botanicals after use. Rinse, dry, and refill the handkerchief with fresh herbs as desired.

April

THE DAFFODIL

D AFFODILS ARE the essence of spring, the happy reveille that signals the garden's full awakening, the surest sign that Nature has traded her winter-white cloak for a mantle of golden blossoms.

I bought my first dozen or so daffodils from a catalog, and from that modest beginning, I now have hundreds. A dainty heirloom narcissus is a wonderful addition to my rock garden, and peach-colored daffodils resembling frilly butterflies make a showy display beneath my deciduous trees. With more than 10,000 cultivars to choose from, I could easily have many more daffodils as permanent guests in my garden. These proven performers return season after season, naturalize happily, and multiply easily. (Another bonus: deer, moles, and mice pass them by.)

I welcome these no-fuss beauties into my home, where they brighten every corner with the brilliance of spring. 'Baby Moon,' a fragrant miniature jonquil, has a special place by my bedside so that I can enjoy its delicate blossoms and scent, up-close. Daffodils are fabulous in cut-flower arrangements. But don't cut the stems; just pull and snap them off at the soil line. Daffodils secrete a sticky sap, so you have to cure them in a vase of warm water for 2 hours before using them in a mixed bouquet.

I think it's impossible to have too many daffodils. A springtime gift to the gardener, these hardy charmers are eager to please, thrive with little or no care, and will flourish for years to come.

"And then my heart with pleasure fills, And dances with the daffodils."
—WILLIAM WORDSWORTH

Planting Tips

Daffodils and jonquils are all members of the genus Narcissus.

Buy plump, firm bulbs. Bulbs with a single nose will have one or two blooms the first year; a double-nose bulb will have more. Choose a combination of early-, mid-, and late-season varieties.

Plant in early fall around the time of the first frost.

Plant in quantity; at least 12 grouped in a border, 50 to 100 for a natural landscape effect.

The Narcissus family prefers well-drained, rich soil.

Do best in full sun but will tolerate light shade.

Dig a hole three times as deep as the height of the bulb and space them apart about three times the width of the bulb.

Mulch newly planted bulbs. Top-dress with a complete fertilizer in the fall when they are forming roots and new bulbs. Do not put fertilizer in the hole with the bulb because new roots may be burned.

After blooms fade, do not braid, cut, or tie foliage; it robs the plant of nutrients. Let foliage die back naturally and turn yellow (about 6 to 8 weeks).

Planting by the Moon

Whenever I tell friends that I'm a lunar gardener, they picture me in the garden at midnight, wearing a long white dress and prancing about barefoot while a full moon illuminates my path with rays of silvery light. And although this fanciful vision appeals to my romantic nature, the art of planting by the moon's phases is quite down to earth and best done in the light of day.

The how-to is simple: During the 2 weeks that the moon is waxing, that is, between the new moon and the full moon, plant annuals and vegetables that bear above ground. Plant biennials, perennials, and root vegetables when the moon is waning, that is, from the day after the full moon to the day before the new moon.

The idea behind this practice is that just as the moon affects the ocean tides, so does it affect the movement of fluids within plants. During the waning of the moon, the sap flows down and invigorates the roots, making this a favorable time for planting or transplanting crops such as carrots and potatoes. When the moon waxes, it draws the sap upward, filling the plants with verve and vim. This interval favors planting crops that mature above ground, like corn and tomatoes.

Naysayers scoff that gardening by the moon's phases is just so much moonshine, but many seasoned gardeners who have exercised a little lunacy have been rewarded with enviable harvests of vibrant flowers, delicious vegetables, and succulent fruit. Whether it's lore or lunatic, linking our gardens to the moon's phases honors the connection between Earth and the heavens.

"Nothing that is can pause or stay; The moon will wax the moon will wane... Tomorrow be today."

—HENRY WADSWORTH LONGFELLOW

Herbs, such as chives (above) and creeping rosemary (below), enhance our lives in a multitude of ways. They have been treasured for their aromatic, culinary, cosmetic, and medicinal virtues. They appeal to cook and gardener alike, and bring pleasure to many dimensions of our lives.

COOK'S HERB GARDEN

 Y FASCINATION with herbs began at a very early age. I remember picking handfuls of basil for my mother and delighting in the heady fragrance that remained on my hands. Years later I am still captivated by the rich perfumes of the herbs in my own garden.

Herbs are easy and rewarding to grow. They can be annuals or perennials, herbaceous or woody, deciduous or evergreen, hardy or tender. Most are naturally pest-resistant, thrive in the ground or in pots, and require minimal care. Just water them regularly until they are established; mulch to hold the moisture in, and pinch them back during the growing season to promote new foliage and bushy growth. Most are not fussy about soil, but since perennial herbs will grow in the same spot for years, enrich poor soils with an annual dose of composted manure. Although there are a few herbs that will thrive in damp, cool shade, the majority prefer sunny, well-drained locales.

Plant List

🍀 **Sweet basil** (*Ocimum basilicum*) is the most common species. Other popular basils include: 'Dark Opal,' 'Purple Ruffles,' and 'Green Ruffles.' Dwarf and scented varieties are available.

🍀 **Rosemary** (*Rosmarinus officinalis*). Cultivars include: 'Corsican,' 'Majorcan Pink,' 'White,' 'Fota Blue,' and 'Golden.' In cold zones rosemary must winter indoors.

🍀 **Mint** (*Mentha*). Spearmint and peppermint, as well as apple, orange, lime, and ginger mints are popular kinds of mint. Mint is rampantly invasive; plant it in containers.

🍀 **Thyme** (*Thymus*). The 300 to 400 species of thyme belong to the mint family. In cold zones, thyme needs winter protection—mulch with pine boughs or set in a cold frame. Common, lemon, and caraway thyme are used for seasoning. Mother-of-thyme, creeping, and woolly thyme are resilient ground covers.

🍀 **Parsley** (*Petroselinum*). Italian, or flat-leaf, parsley is intensely flavorful and preferred for culinary uses. French, or curly-leaf, parsley is best used as a garnish.

COMPANION PLANTING

"Though an old man, I am but a young gardener."

—THOMAS JEFFERSON

RIENDSHIPS flourish in the plant kingdom as much as they do among the animals. Knowing which alliances to encourage—and which to discourage—will benefit the busy gardener. Some plant pairs form a natural defense against pests and disease. For example, when planted in close proximity, asparagus plants help protect tomatoes from nematodes and tomatoes return the favor by warding off asparagus beetles. I also plant marigolds among my tomatoes; the flowers add flashes of sunshiny brilliance and help keep the vegetables free from pests. Nasturtiums will keep aphids away from broccoli and squash. Other relationships are literally nourishing—one plant enhances the growth of other plants. Chives improve the health of roses and carrots, and marjoram in the garden is beneficial to almost all vegetables, improving both their vigor and flavor.

Not all pairings are benevolent, however. Some plants are ill-suited for each other simply because they compete for the same nutrients, water, and light. Sunflowers and pole beans are an undesirable combination for this reason. Other plants emit irritating or toxic root secretions into the soil to the detriment of another plant. The roots of black walnut trees secrete a noxious substance, and plants such as peas, peppers, tomatoes, potatoes, and blueberries should be planted a distance from this tree.

Learning these needs of your plants will help you grow a healthier, more productive garden.

Planting Tips

PLANT	COMPANIONS
Carrots	Likes: Chives, leeks, lettuce, onions, peas, radishes, tomatoes. Rosemary and sage help repel carrot fly. Dislikes: Dill, fennel.
Cucumbers	Likes: Beans, lettuce, peas. Corn for protection against wilt virus. Sunflowers for shade. Dislikes: Potatoes, aromatic herbs (e.g., mint, sage, thyme).
Lettuce	Likes: Beets, radishes, strawberries. Chervil and dill protect against aphids. Dislikes: Broccoli, fava beans.
Mint	Attracts beneficial insects. Repels ants, fleas, rodents. (Plant in containers, roots are invasive.)
Peas	Likes: Corn, cucumbers, eggplant, radishes. Dislikes: Chives, garlic, leeks, onions.
Peppers	Likes: Basil, marjoram, nasturtium, oregano, tansy. Dislikes: Fennel.
Radishes	Likes: Bush and pole beans, chervil, lettuces, mustard, nasturtium, peas.
Roses	Likes: Tomatoes protect from black spot. Marigolds help to repel nematodes. Garlic, onions, and chives fight aphids and black spot. Parsley, thyme, geraniums and catnip also helpful.
Strawberries	Likes: Borage, lettuce, spinach.
Tomatoes	Likes: Asparagus, basil, parsley, sage, carrots, chives, garlic, onions. Borage helps repel hornworms. Marigolds and nasturtiums protect against aphids. Garlic protects against red spider mites. Roses help increase fruit yield, improve resistance to verticillium wilt. Dislikes: Potatoes, fennel.
Zucchini	Likes: Corn, mint, nasturtium, radishes.

SPRING FESTIVITIES

SPRING BRINGS with it various enriching holy days, and if the weather permits, I celebrate Easter with an outdoor buffet. Homemade decorations include a tree of spring branches hung with moss-covered "eggs." Real eggs, colored with dyes derived from yellow onion skins, blueberries, and beets, fill a nearby wire stand. Candles glow beside violets and lilies on the egg stand, terracotta pots and worn wooden boxes sport lush "lawns," and topiaries of rosemary and ivy complete the lighthearted accouterments.

FLORAL WREATH

THROUGHOUT the ages wreaths have served as symbols of the ever-changing cycle of nature. Just as an autumn wreath of wheat signifies that season's bounty, so a floral wreath signifies spring's rebirth. Easter is a celebration of renewal and hope, and a wreath replete with floral splendors is a natural embellishment for this special day.

Whether you are celebrating a wedding, a graduation, or an anniversary, or simply hosting a dinner party, a floral wreath is a wonderful expression of the joy of the occasion. It will liven up a ho-hum table or convey a hospitable greeting when displayed in a window or hung on the front door. Wreaths can be more than an expression of personal esteem. When your wreath reflects your own style and personality it will enrich and enhance whatever celebration it graces.

There is no need to wait until Christmas to try your hand at wreath-making. If you are a lover of flowers, you will enjoy creating your very own springtime floral fantasy.

"Proud-pied April,
dressed all in trim
Hath put a spirit
of youth in
everything."
—WILLIAM
SHAKESPEARE

Materials

- Florist's foam, such as Oasis
- 16-inch (40-cm) diameter wire form
- Florist's wire or tape
- Sheet moss or decoration moss
- Florist's pins
- 36 Roses (or other stiff-stemmed flowers)
- 10 Lilies, such as 'Star Gazer,' 'Montreux,' or 'Le Reve'
- 10 Alstroemeria, such as 'Jacqueline', 'Othello', or 'Manon'
- Clippers

Cover work surface with plastic and newspaper. Saturate florist's foam with warm water. Place wire form on work surface and fill with wet foam. Wrap florist's wire or tape around form to secure foam. Wrap moss around rim; secure with florist's pins. Trim flower stems to about 2 inches (5cm). Space roses evenly over the wire form, gently pushing stems into the foam. Work from the center out; then fill in with other flowers. If you use the wreath as a centerpiece, protect the table with a waterproof material; if you hang it, let the water drain first. Spray flowers with a plant mister as needed to refresh them.

VERSATILE HERBS

ERBS ARE natural flavor enhancers. When combined with the rich taste of butter, they are indulgently delicious on a baked potato, tossed in a bowl of pasta—even melted over popcorn. Flavored butters are easy to make and will keep in the freezer for as long as 2 months. Try them with grilled meats, fish, steamed vegetables, or crusty bread.

For special occasions, use cookie cutters to form cheerful shapes. Chill the flavored butter, place it between two pieces of waxed paper, and roll it out until it is about 1/4 inch (6mm) thick. Press out desired shapes and top them with herb sprigs or edible flowers to make each pat a delight to the eye as well as to the taste buds.

Herb Butters

Pesto Butter: 1 cup (60g) firmly packed fresh basil leaves

2 medium-size garlic cloves, minced

1/4 cup flat-leaf parsley

2 sticks (8 ounces/230g) unsalted butter, softened

1/2 teaspoon salt

1/4 teaspoon freshly ground pepper

Thyme/Lemon Butter: 4 tablespoons fresh thyme leaves

2 sticks (8 ounces/230g) unsalted butter, softened

1 teaspoon grated lemon rind

1 teaspoon fresh lemon juice

1/2 teaspoon salt

1/4 teaspoon freshly ground pepper

In a food processor, mince herbs. (For Pesto Butter, mince basil, garlic, and parsley; for Thyme-Lemon Butter, mince thyme leaves.) Add softened butter and remaining recipe ingredients, then process until blended. Spoon butter mixture onto a 12-inch (30-cm) length of wax paper and roll it to form a log 1 1/2 inches (4cm) thick. Twist the ends of the paper to secure the form; chill in the refrigerator for at least 2 hours. Before serving, bring butter to room temperature. Yield: approximately one cup (250g) each.

HERB SEASONING

I T'S TIME TO head to the garden to snip some herbs. The flavors of freshly picked herbs are subtler and more delicate than those of dried herbs. And, happily, growing a number of different delectable herbs does not require an especially green thumb or acres of property. Herbs will thrive in pots and window boxes, so busy cooks can easily have a ready supply at their fingertips to use in all their favorite dishes. Bouquet garni (literally "garnished bouquet"), a staple seasoning in classic French cooking, is comprised of a small bundle of fresh or dried herbs that is added to stews, soups, stocks, and slow-roasted meats to enhance their natural flavors.

Bouquet garni

2 or 3 sprigs fresh parsley

1 or 2 sprigs fresh thyme

1 or 2 bay leaves
(Use dried leaves, fresh can be bitter.)

To make one bouquet garni, wrap the herbs in a square of cheesecloth and tie the bundle with plain white kitchen string. Add to simmering pot. Remove before serving or storing food.

"To have nothing but Sweet Herbs, and those only choice ones too, and every kind its bed by itself."
—Desiderius Erasmus

HERBAL MOTH CHASERS

HAVE FOND memories of my grandmother placing pomanders awash with lavender in her closets, but the practice of using herbs to discourage moths is centuries old. Southernwood was used so extensively in 18th-century France that its common name was *garde-robe*. One need not be a linguist to understand the translation. Rosemary, mint, feverfew, and tansy can also guard your out-of-season wardrobe.

Lovely old-fashioned sachets composed of these natural herbs and spices add pleasant aromas and decorative touches to your closets, chests, armoires, and suitcases. Lavender balls look and smell heavenly and are particularly well-suited for tucking among lingerie and linens.

Preparation

Sachet: 8 cups mixed crushed spices and dried leaves and herbs, such as feverfew, lavender, mint, rosemary, santolina, southernwood, tansy, or wormwood

1 tablespoon whole cloves

1 cinnamon stick, broken into 2 inch (5cm) pieces

Decorative fabric made into four 8 inch x 4 inch (20cm x 10cm) sacks

Ribbon

Mix herbs and spices in a ceramic or glass bowl. Cover the bowl and store it in a cool dark place for about two weeks to allow mixture to mature. Divide the herb-spice mixture among the 4 sacks and close each with a ribbon tie. Yield: 4 sachets

Lavender Balls: 4-inch (10-cm) Styrofoam ball

All-purpose craft glue

1-inch (3-cm) paintbrush

1 cup of dried lavender florets

Ribbon

Spread glue over ball with brush; one section at a time. Roll ball in lavender florets pressing lavender to glue as you proceed; you may need to repeat in certain areas for total coverage. Tie with ribbon. Yield: one ball

"All overgrown with azure moss, and flowers So sweet, the sense faints picturing them!"

—Percy Bysshe Shelley

May

THE TULIP

ONTEMPORARY speculators invest in stocks, bonds, or works of art, but in 17th-century Holland, speculators bought and sold tulip bulbs. Introduced into Vienna in the 1550s, the original stock came from varieties that grew wild in western and central Asia. A botanist brought a few bulbs to the Netherlands, where eager breeding and collecting created tulipomania, a frenzy that held the country in its grip for years. Spectacular fortunes were made and lost by trading this exotic bulb, and prices eventually exceeded those of precious metals. Tulip fervor hit fever pitch in 1636 when a single bulb of a highly sought-after streaked variety sold for the sum of 5,500 florins (approximately $2,500 in today's currency).

Unfortunately, the attractive streaking was caused by a virus carried by insects which weakened and destroyed the plant. Prices toppled, the tulip

"The gardens fire with a joyful blaze Of tulips in the mornings' rays."
—RALPH WALDO EMERSON

market collapsed, and many traders were left in ruin. In time, the virus was identified and eradicated, but it took years for Holland to recover from tulipomania.

Meanwhile, the passion and enthusiasm for this stately flower flourished throughout the world. In Victorian England bold swains sent red tulips as an unspoken but unmistakable statement of their true love. The Germans who immigrated to Pennsylvania planted tulips in the fertile valleys where they settled. To this day a stylized tulip blossom is a characteristic emblem in their handicrafts.

Tulips continue to charm us with their timeless beauty and extraordinary range of sizes, shapes, and colors. Tall or tiny, feathered or fringed, solid or streaked—tulips are the crowning glory of a spring garden.

Planting Tips

Although classed with perennials, tulips often need to be treated as annuals. When the foliage has died back, dig up the bulbs and store them in a cool, dry, airy place until autumn, then replant. Many hybrids will not bloom well after the first or second spring; shrinking blossoms indicate that new bulbs are needed. Wild, or species, tulips such as *Tulipa clusiana, T. turkestanica* and *T. tarda* are true perennials. Only 3 to 8 inches (7 to 10cm) high, they are hardier than the hybrids, easier to maintain as perennials, and will generally increase every year. Plant bulbs in masses; for an extended blooming season, buy species or cultivars with early-, mid-, and late-season flowering times.

🍃 Choose firm bulbs with no scars or black spots.

🍃 Plant in autumn, before the ground freezes. Tulips should be the last spring bulbs to go into the ground.

🍃 Well-drained soil is essential; add compost or sand if needed to improve drainage. Tulips that get too wet are susceptible to disease.

🍃 Plant tulips deep—6 to 8 inches (15 to 20cm) deep—and spaced about 6 inches (15cm) apart.

🍃 After planting, water well and cover with 2 inches (5cm) of dry mulch such as wood chips or salt hay.

🍃 Plant in full sun or light shade. Avoid windy places; wind can damage the flowers.

🍃 Fertilize at planting time with a fertilizer made especially for bulbs. Fertilize again when shoots appear in spring.

🍃 Deadhead spent flowers, clip just below the flower. Do not remove foliage until it is completely brown.

Plant List

Purchase virus-free plants from reliable nurseries or mail-order suppliers.

🍀 June-bearing. Plant these in the spring for fruit the next year. This variety produces one crop in June and July. As the days become longer and warmer, June-bearers stop flowering and start making runners. At the end of the runners are plants that will flower and fruit the following year.

🍀 Everbearing. Each year, ever-bearing strawberries yield two crops: one large crop in June and a smaller crop in late summer or early autumn. Flowers form during the long, hot days of summer. Replace the plants about every 3 years.

🍀 Day-neutral. For plants that flower and fruit continuously for about 4 months choose day-neutrals. They produce fewer runners than other varieties and should be replaced about every 2 years.

🍀 Alpine. These primarily run-nerless plants produce tiny, tasty berries from summer until frost.

HOMEGROWN STRAWBERRIES

 UCCULENT strawberries are one of the great delights of a home garden. They are among the easiest fruits to grow and will produce a large amount of fruit from a relatively small planting—a bonus for space-conscious gardeners. Strawberries will thrive in containers such as a traditional strawberry pot or a large tub or barrel as happily as they do in the ground. I plant them in my rock garden where the green foliage, white flowers, and red berries make a handsome—and delicious—edging. Ever-congenial, strawberries mingle well with herbs as well as flowers and other ornamental plants.

"Doubtless God could have made a better berry, but doubtless God never did."

—Dr. William Butler

Plant strawberries 12 to 15 inches (30 to 40cm) apart in rich, well-drained, slightly acid soil and full sun. Use a dry mulch to deter weeds. If you live in a cold area (temperatures at or below 20°F (7°C), cover the plants with 3 to 6 inches (8 to 15cm) of clean straw or pine needles after a hard frost and before air temperatures remain below freezing. Remove the mulch gradually in spring, when the threat of frost has passed.

Most plantings will produce berries for 3 to 4 years. When the yield and size of the berries decreases, replace the bed. Set out new plants in a new location to fight insect and disease problems. Select an assortment of varieties, and you'll be rewarded with a months-long supply of fruit.

BUTTERFLY GARDEN

REATING A hospitable garden for butterflies (and for caterpillars) brings many benefits. I coax these beauties into my garden with a delectable array of leafy and nectar-rich plants and with flowering shrubs that provide shelter from wind and bad weather. Flat rocks, judiciously placed to absorb heat from the sun, attract a bevy of baskers. A shallow puddle or pan filled with sand and water has frequent visitors, particularly males who are attracted to these sites by minerals in the sand.

Floating from flower to flower, butterflies lend a little magic to our lives and repay simple kindnesses by multiplying the flower population with their superb pollinating skills.

"Butterfly, flower, and my eyes are one."

—MOBI HO

Plant List

To safeguard butterfly larvae, avoid using pesticides in your garden. Plant an assortment of butterfly-friendly flowers to ensure successive blooming and a steady diet from early spring through fall.

Host Plants for Caterpillars

🍀 Butterfly weed, carrot, clover, dill, fennel, milkweed, nettle, parsley, passionflower, Queen Anne's lace, rue, spicebush, thistle, violet

Nectar Plants for Butterflies

🍀 Annuals: Cosmos, heliotrope, impatiens, lantana, marigold, snapdragon, flowering tobacco, zinnia
🍀 Perennials: Aster, bee balm, black-eyed Susan, coreopsis, phlox, purple coneflower
🍀 Wildflowers: Butterfly weed, clover, Joe Pye weed, milkweed, Queen Anne's lace, thistle
🍀 Vines: Dutchman's pipe, honeysuckle, passionflower, scarlet runner bean, trumpet vine
🍀 Herbs: Catnip, chives, lavender, mint
🍀 Shrubs: Azalea, butterfly bush, privet, rhododendron, viburnum

MINIATURE GARDEN

 SMALL-SCALE garden is ideal for introducing children to gardening's pleasures. But grownups also respond to the small garden's charm. A pint-size planting is a thoughtful gift for an apartment dweller or for someone with limited mobility who enjoys growing things. All you need is a container, some soil, a few dwarf species plants, and *voila!* —an instant garden.

The main thing to keep in mind when planting a portable plot is to choose plants that have similar light, soil, water, and fertilization needs. Many small-leaf herbs, such as creeping myrtle, thyme, oregano, and rosemary, are well-suited to an indoor garden. An assortment of cacti and other succulents, such as *Crassula Echeveria,* or *Sempervivum,* or of alpine plants such as *Saxifraga, Ramonda,* and *Haberlea* are enchanting and do well in small places.

Materials

- Wooden crate or box
- Plastic trash bag
- Gravel
- Sterile potting soil
- Assorted alpines, succulents, or small-leaf herbs
- Assorted decorations, such as pebbles, shells, miniature benches and gardening utensils

Line the wooden crate with the plastic trash bag. Fill the crate one-third full with gravel; add potting soil to within 1/2 inch (1.5cm) of the rim. Spread pebbles to create a path or other design. Install plants. Decorate as desired with miniature benches and gardening utensils. Use shells for birdbaths.

TUSSIE-MUSSIE

URING the Victorian era the nosegay, once used to distract the bearer from offensive odors, took on a more romantic and elegant identity. Proper etiquette of the day dictated that well-dressed ladies and gentlemen wear or carry a tussie-mussie. ("Tussie" referred to the clusters of flowers and "mussie" to the moss that kept them fresh.)

Because of the Victorians' popular "language of flowers," a tussie-mussie often communicated a coded message. One can only guess how many ardent suitors proclaimed undying love with nosegays of scarlet tulips in hand. Today, a tussie-mussie remains a charming and sentimental way to express affection to brides, mothers, graduates, and friends.

Materials

🌺 Fresh or dried flowers and herbs

🌺 Sheet moss

🌺 Florist's tape

🌺 Lace, paper doily, or posy holder

Choose a primary flower for the center. Trim the stem to about 6 inches (15cm) and remove bottom leaves. Dampen the moss. (This will not be necessary if you are using dried botanicals or if the nosegay will be kept in water.) Working in concentric circles, surround the center flower with other flowers and herbs, using florist's tape to secure the bouquet. Try to keep the top symmetrical. Wrap the stem with damp moss and cover it with more florist's tape. Insert stem into posy holder, through a hole in a lace doily, or wrap it with lace, ribbon, and streamers.

> "The flowers put forth
> their precious odors, And
> none can tell how from so small
> a centre come such sweets."
>
> —WILLIAM BLAKE

HERBAL FACIAL STEAM

AN HERBAL FACIAL steam is a stimulating treat for your skin. Enjoying the benefits of aromatherapy while in the garden further enhances the pleasure of this beauty treatment. The combination of fragrant herbs, fresh air, and singing birds makes this a blissful treat for the mind, body, and spirit. (If your skin is sensitive or delicate, it is advisable to forgo this treatment; people with asthma or respiratory allergies should consult their physicians before using.)

Preparation

3 to 4 cups of steaming-hot water

1 cup of mixed fresh herbs, whole or snipped

Large towel

Combine the leaves and flowers of 2 or more of the following to make 1 cup: calendula, chamomile, comfrey, lady's mantle, lavender, mint, rose petals, rosemary, sage, or yarrow. Place herbs in a large ceramic bowl. Pour steaming water into the bowl and let the herbs steep for about a minute. Hold your face about 10 inches (25cm) above the water; tent the towel over your head and the bowl so that the vapors don't escape. Close your eyes, breathe deeply, and relax for 5 to 10 minutes. Rinse your face with cool or tepid water, pat dry, and moisturize.

BURSTING WITH **BERRIES**

ITH THE advent of warmer weather, I find myself caught in spring's most consuming passion —the search for luscious, succulent berries. The sight of plump strawberries, fragile raspberries, velvety blueberries, and fat juicy blackberries has me wishing for a longer harvest season. Eaten alone, straight from the vine, berries are one of nature's sweetest dividends. They not only look and taste good but also are quite good for you. The intoxicating fragrances, tantalizing flavors, and jewel-like colors of just-picked berries provide endless inspiration for delectable recipes. So indulge and enjoy!

Berry Bread Pudding

1 quart (580g/4 cups) fresh blueberries

1/3 cup (67g) sugar

Finely grated zest of 1 lemon

Juice of 1/2 lemon

6 to 8 thick slices of French bread or similar amount of brioche

2 tablespoons unsalted butter, softened

2 tablespoons dark brown sugar

1 teaspoon cinnamon

Preheat oven to 375°F (190°C). Generously butter a 10-inch (25-cm) baking dish. In a large bowl, mix berries, sugar, lemon zest, and lemon juice. Place mixture into buttered baking dish and bake until the berries are soft (10 to 15 minutes). While fruit mixture is baking, butter one side of each piece of bread or brioche. Remove fruit mixture from oven. Arrange bread or brioche over the fruit, buttered side up. Mix brown sugar and cinnamon in a small bowl; sprinkle over bread and entire fruit mixture. Return dish to oven and bake for 15 to 20 minutes. Fruit should be bubbly and the top browned. Cool briefly. Serve with heavy cream or ice cream. Serves 6.

Strawberry-Blueberry Sauce

1 pint (300g/2 cups, sliced) strawberries, hulled

1 pint (290g/2 cups) blueberries

1/4 cup (50g) sugar

1 tablespoon fresh lemon juice

Place half the strawberries in a medium-size bowl, crush them with a fork. Slice remaining strawberries and add to the bowl. Add half the blueberries. Place the remaining blueberries in a saucepan with the sugar and lemon juice. Stir over moderate heat until sugar dissolves and juice becomes syrupy (about 3 minutes). Add to strawberry mixture. Cool and serve over frozen yogurt or angel food cake. Yield: approximately 3 cups (750ml).

"The Spirits of the Air live on the smells Of fruit; and Joy, with pinions light, roves round the gardens, or sits singing in the trees."

—WILLIAM BLAKE

"Not only the days, but life itself lengthens in summer. I would... gather more of it to me, could I do so."

—RICHARD JEFFRIES

Summer

SIMPLY SUMMER

SUMMER MAKES me giddy. It enters with an ethereal waltz of cool pastel foxgloves, peonies, and delphiniums, and exits in a brilliant tango of hot-toned sunflowers, zinnias, and black-eyed Susans. In between is a profusion of sights, sounds, and scents—beds and borders overflowing with an array of flowers, trees and trellises laden with fruit ripe for picking, vegetables ready for harvest. Bright-winged birds splash playfully in the birdbath while butterflies glide from blossom to blossom, gathering nectar.

Summer's particular music builds on birdsong and the industrious hum of honeybees, and rises on the breezes that dance through the rich green leaves on the trees. It follows the steady beat of crickets chirping and the syncopation of squirrels busy chattering, chattering, chattering.

There is a special magic to this time—mornings fresh with dew, afternoons ablaze with the sun's warmth, and evenings filled with the drowsy aromas of jasmine, moonflower, and honeysuckle. The special scents of summer revive memories of carefree summers past. One whiff of cut grass and I'm transported back to the 60s, watching Dad in his tropical floral shirt mowing the lawn at breakneck speed, hoping to steal away for a round of golf. If ever my nose chances upon the glorious, unmistakable fragrance of gardenias, I am unfailingly reminded of my mother, hat and gloves on and ready for a special outing with my sister and me.

For summer is, above all, an Escape from Routine. Some mornings I can be found in my robe gathering flowers still glistening with dew. The birds are trilling, the air is fragrant, the sun is smiling gently, its beams not yet strong enough to supplant the night's chill with the day's warmth. There is peace and tranquillity in the garden at this hour in this season, a harmony that soothes and uplifts my spirit. It is a time for the gardener to enjoy the rewards of the year's loving labors, to celebrate and savor all the joys and blessings of this bountiful season.

"Summer afternoon, summer afternoon, to me those have always been the two most beautiful words in the English language."
—HENRY JAMES

A Summer Outing

Greenmarkets, farm stands, and farmers' markets are a living link to our agrarian past, a celebration of the season, and one of the absolute joys of high summer. Take the time to discover your local markets and farm stands. The wagons there overflow with a delectable abundance of just-picked delights—sweet corn, vine-ripened tomatoes, plump berries, musky melons, and luscious peaches, armloads of field flowers, fresh herbs, and healthful leafy greens—that even the most urban of visitors couldn't resist.

THINGS TO DO

🌿 After the soil has warmed up, mulch plants to keep roots cool, conserve moisture in the soil, and keep weeds down. To prevent fungus, don't let the mulch touch the plants' stems.

🌿 In warmer climates move house-plants outdoors to a partially shaded area of the garden or porch.

🌿 Remove spent flowers from spring-blooming perennials.

🌿 Wait for the foliage on spring bulbs to turn yellow and die back before removing it. The gradual lessening of foliage is a sign that the bulbs are storing strength for the next season.

🌿 Prune and feed early-flowering shrubs after they finish blooming.

🌿 Inspect roses for insects, mildew, blackspot, and rust. Spray with an appropriate fungicide (check the label) when signs first appear. Pick Japanese beetles off roses and spray aphids with insecticidal soap.

🌿 When deadheading rose blossoms, cut back to first stem with five leaflets.

"But to the Gard'ners care
These things we leave;
they are his Business,
With setting flowers and
planting fruitful Trees"
—JOHN EVELYN

Middle

❧ Pinch back asters and chrysanthemums to encourage fuller plants for fall blooming.

❧ Cut excess growth on any wisteria after it finishes flowering.

❧ Plant late-blooming perennials in pots outdoors.

❧ Harvest lettuce and replant bed with vegetables that produce later in the season, such as carrots, chinese cabbage, or radishes.

❧ Remove spent flowers from bearded irises. Every third year, dig up the rhizomes and discard the old soft growth in the center. Remove strong rhizomes on the sides and replant them with the upper part of the rhizomes slightly above the soil.

Late

❧ In early August sow any of the following for fall harvest: beets, kale, endive, spinach, and turnips.

❧ In early August perennial seedlings will be sturdy enough to thin out and transplant for autumn blooming.

❧ Order spring bulbs for fall planting.

Ongoing

❧ Remove faded blossoms from annuals and perennials to keep them blooming all summer.

❧ Feed annuals, roses, and other heavy bloomers. (In colder regions feed roses for the last time in August.)

❧ Snip basil and other herbs to encourage bushy growth.

❧ Use stakes to support floppy or tall-growing plants such as lilies, delphiniums, and dahlias.

❧ Stake and tie tomato plants. Keep tying them as they grow. Feed once a week and pinch off any suckers that sprout between the main stem and a leaf stem.

❧ Train cucumbers and other vines or climbers to grow on fences or trellises.

❧ Remember to water plants in containers frequently, or they will dry out.

❧ Harvest flowers, vegetables, and herbs early or late in the day.

❧ Lie in a hammock and read a good book!

THE GARDEN HABITAT

 **W**ELCOMING WILDLIFE into our gardens by providing inviting habitats—food, water, and nesting materials in the form of annuals, perennials, trees, shrubs, and vines—yields personal as well as global benefits. Our hearts are gladdened to see birds and butterflies, dragonflies and fireflies, green lacewings, bright ladybugs, and the ever-busy bees darting about the garden. And our spirits are lifted knowing that their industry helps keep the ecosystem in balance.

 Birds, especially hummingbirds, devour flies, moths, slugs, cutworms, and mosquitoes along with their eggs and larva. Hummers are attracted to red, pink, and orange tubular flowers (such as trumpet vines and cardinal flowers) but you can attract a variety of avian natives by planting thistle, Virginia creeper, honeysuckle, dogwood, viburnum, sunflower, aster, salvia, cosmos, and zinnia. Include some pyracantha, bittersweet, or holly for welcome winter food.

Hummingbirds help to pollinate plants, but the true monarchs in that realm are the butterflies and bees. Butterflies need to keep warm in order to fly; a few flat rocks set in a sunny spot will give them a reliable place to rest and recharge. Tuck a shallow water pan in a secluded spot and keep it filled. Encourage butterflies by providing host plants for caterpillars (butterfly weed, parsley, dill, Queen Anne's lace and milkweed, for example) as well as nectar-rich blossoms for food. Heliotrope, phlox, lantana, aster, butterfly bush, purple coneflower, coreopsis, and black-eyed Susan are irresistible lures for these winged garden jewels.

Bumblebees do not produce honey, but they are important to cold-zone gardeners because they start pollinating early in the season. All bees need a continuous supply of pollen and nectar. To keep them coming back for repeat visits, plant beds that include campanula, delphinium, echinops, monarda, scabiosa, malva, nigella, or veronica. Bees also love mint plants, lemon balm, sweet basil, lavender, and thyme. Tree fruit is a favorite no matter what the species, raspberries, blackberries, and alpine strawberries, are also appealing to bees.

*"He who shares the joy
in what he's grown
spreads joy abroad and
doubles his own."*
—ANONYMOUS

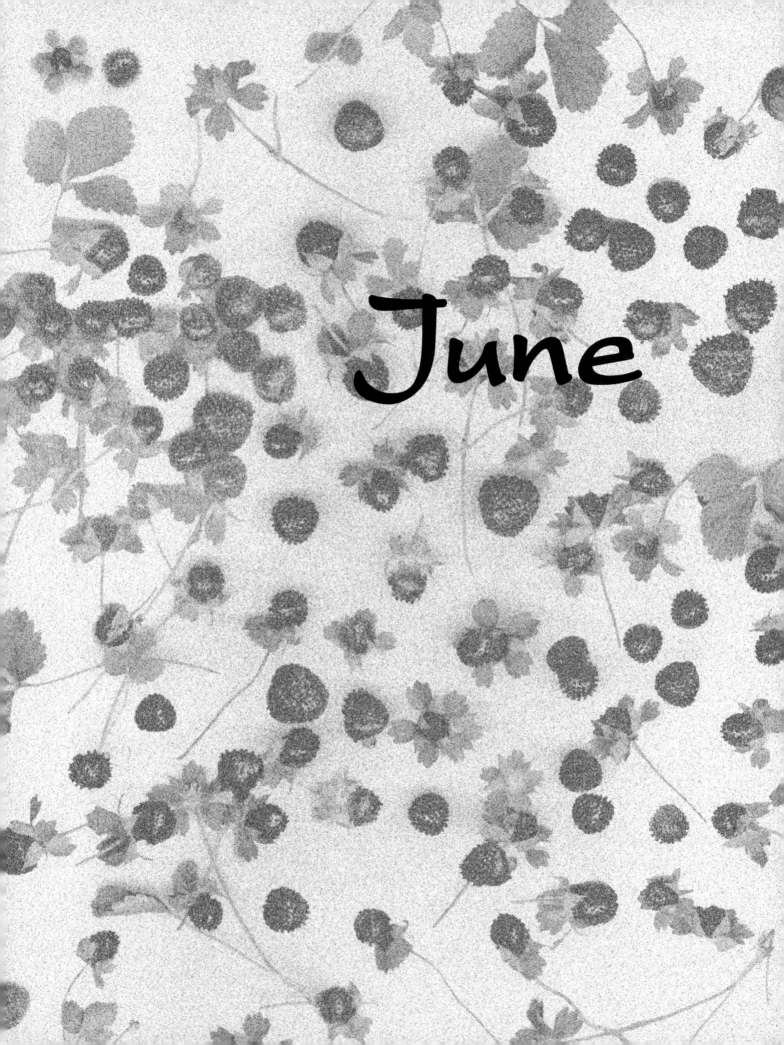

June

THE ROSE

HE IMMORTAL rose. Is it possible to be human, to be alive, and remain untouched by this special flower? I think not. Its captivating fragrance, sumptuous blossoms, and dazzling colors have made this queen of flowers a symbol of love throughout history.

My own love of antique roses is bound up with memories of my grandmother, Nonna. She was one of many immigrants who, during the great wave of migration from Europe, carried a living reminder of the homeland she left behind. Nonna brought a rose bush with her on the arduous transatlantic voyage.

Nonna's roses were her pride and joy. Caring for them gave her enormous pleasure, and I spent many a day tagging after her in her garden. My grandmother was not a collector of material things, nor did she acquire many valuables. She did have a good watch, antique earrings, and a string of pearls. Every memory I have of Nonna in her garden is of her wearing

"We bring roses, beautiful fresh roses, dewey as the morning and colored like Dawn."

—Thomas Buchanan Read

her pearls and one of the many pretty floral aprons that were basic to her wardrobe.

Today many of us spend our lives in perpetual fast forward. I often look back on the time spent with my grandmother and appreciate how many of life's lessons were learned in her garden. Nonna possessed grace and dignity. And I find that tending the descendants of her beloved roses in my own garden helps keep her legacy alive.

Planting Tips

- Slightly acidic soil (a pH between 6.0 and 6.5).
- Bright light, at least 6 hours a day of full, direct sun (morning sun, if possible).
- Fertilizer. Make three light applications of fertilizer throughout the season: once when growth begins, once after the first bloom, and once 6 weeks later. (But stop all feeding 6 weeks before the first frost.)
- Water. Approximately 1 inch of water a week. Water the ground, not the plant; splashing promotes diseases, insects, and mold.
- Good drainage. Roses do not like wet feet.
- Pest prevention. To protect against aphids, interplant roses with members of the allium family— garlic, onions, chives, or shallots.
- Disease prevention. To protect against mildew and black spot, spray roses once a week with a solution of 1 tablespoon of baking soda, 1 tablespoon of ultra-fine horticultural spray oil, and 1 gallon (4l) of water.
- Epsom salts (*magnesium sulfate*) promotes new growth and keeps the leaves from turning yellow. In the spring, I sprinkle a few tablespoons of Epsom salts around the base of my rose bushes, gently scratch it into the soil with a rake, and water it in.

PERENNIALS for a SHADE GARDEN

WO GRAND copper beech trees, each more than 100 years old, create a graceful entrance to my garden. Their branches, heavy with penny-colored leaves, are a cool haven for a hardworking gardener, but a hazard for the sun-loving plants I knew and loved so well.

Even thinking the word "shade" filled me with dismay, and I tried—more than once—to grow a variety of sun-worshiping plants in that spot. The plants withered and my frustration soared. After 2 years of trial and error I came to terms with the reality of my sun-deprived area and discovered a whole new and exciting world of plants—beautiful herbaceous plants—that thrive in what I had called adverse conditions.

The plants you select must be adaptable to the quality of shade that will become home to them. Begin with the question: What kind of shade do I have anyway? Is it full, light, partial, dappled, heavy, or filtered? You must also factor in whether the shade is constant or moves with the sun, whether it fluctuates by season—as it does under my deciduous beeches—and whether it is moist or dry.

On a scorching summer day, a shade garden provides a cooling respite, a soothing invitation to be at one with nature. The informal composition of a shade garden is really much more in harmony with nature than most other types of gardens. Now I proudly usher guests into the cool tranquillity of my shade garden and it is my hope that other contemporary gardeners will find a similar enriching experience and joy in gardening in the shade.

Plant List

In spring, before the leaves appear on the trees, you can grow a colorful array of crocuses, daffodils, hyacinths, and tulips interplanted with other early bloomers such as forget-me-nots and Virginia bluebells. Dappled sunlight, cast by the trees' young leaves, is ideal for Solomon's seal, bleeding hearts, and columbines.

As spring moves gently into summer, foxgloves, and astilbes bloom bravely in the deepening shadows. From midsummer to late fall, monkshoods shoot up tall spikes topped with their characteristic hooded, purplish-blue flowers.

Ferns add a delicate, graceful quality to a shade corner and help to fill in open areas. And there are any number of hostas—more than 1,000 cultivars—for any number of uses in the garden.

Shade-loving perennials include bleeding heart (above), and hostas (right). Bleeding heart will thrive in woodland soil, hostas generally prefer a moist environment.

FRAGRANCE in the GARDEN

UDYARD KIPLING once wrote, "Smells are surer than sights and sounds to make your heartstrings crack." How very true! I am a hopeless romantic and the enticing aroma of lilacs never fails to beckon to me. A much-anticipated time of year for friends is when my lilies of the valley bloom. These plants multiply prodigiously so I dig them up and pot them as gifts. The reaction is always the same—a whiff, a sigh, and a heartfelt thank-you.

If fragrance is as important to you as it is to me, guarantee year-round indulgence by planting a variety of flowers, herbs, vines, trees, and shrubs. Make certain that you choose scented varieties when you buy your plants. Alas, many "new and improved" strains have had their fragrance bred right out of them in favor of resistance to disease, and some plant families noted for their fragrance have scentless varieties.

Whenever I hear about a particularly fragrant bulb cultivar, I jot its name down in my gardening notebook so that I don't forget it or become overwhelmed at the nursery (and base my choices on the appeal of the photograph on the package). Remember to include a few plants that practice their seduction as night falls; flowering tobacco (*Nicotiana sylvestris* or *N. alata*) and moonflower (*Ipomoea alba*) are two that release their perfume at dusk.

Plant List

🦋 The year of the scented garden begins in early spring with flowering bulbs. The heady scent of hyacinth wafts sweetly from *Hyacinthus orientalis*. Grape hyacinths, such as *Muscari azureum, M. botryoides*, and *M. comosum*, offer a more delicate aroma. Fragrant jonquils include 'Suzy' and 'Quail,' for daffodils plant 'Thalia' and 'Carlton,' for tulips, 'Angelique,' 'Apricot Beauty,' and 'Bellona.'

🦋 Aromatic annuals include heliotropes, sweet peas, and sweet alyssums (*Lobularia maritima*). Perennial choices abound. Dianthus, sweet lavender, phlox, lilies, and scented geraniums offer a wide range of flowery, fruity, and spicy scents. Clematis and wisterias are fragrant climbers. And the classic perfume of roses is reborn in heirloom types from the Damask, Moss, Alba, and Bourbon groups.

🦋 Indoors, pots of kitchen herbs such as rosemary, sage, or mint will release their homey aromas all year. Outdoors, plant resilient herbs like chamomile or thyme between the stones in a garden path to make every step a fragrant treat.

Install plants where their fragrance is certain to be enjoyed—in a window box, next to a door, beside a favorite bench, or along a walkway.

CUTTING GARDEN

LOWERS ARE at the top of my Life's Simple Joys list. And when you pick a bouquet from your own garden you give yourself a gift that remains with you throughout the day, and beyond.

A cutting garden does not need a great amount of space nor even its own space. Almost any patch of land or cache of pots can serve. The key to maintaining a steady supply of blooms is deadheading: pinching or clipping faded blossoms from the stem. Deadheading encourages the plant to produce more flowers instead of going to seed. I pick my flowers in the morning when they are at their peak, before the midday sun has had time to dry them out.

Beautiful flowers deserve sparkling clean, bacteria-free containers. I wash mine thoroughly with a solution of 10 parts water to 1 part bleach, then rinse with plenty of plain, fresh water. The vase life of your flowers will be extended if you cut the stems at a diagonal with pruning shears, immediately immerse the cut stems up to their necks in tepid water (roses

Plant List

♣ Showy perennials are excellent for cutting; they include astilbes, bearded irises, columbines, lavenders, black-eyed Susans, pincushion flowers, asters, coneflowers, Shasta daisies, delphiniums, and yarrows. Such annuals as zinnias, cosmos, verbenas, salvias, and snapdragons are good selections for a "cut-again" garden. Include some flowers that dry well—cockscomb or globe amaranth, for example—and you'll have a year-round reminder of summer's extravagance.

prefer warm water), then leave them in a cool and shaded area for several hours. If the flower has a hollow stem, hold it upside down, fill the stem with water, then seal it with a piece of cotton. Florists remove thorns from roses to avoid injuries; leave yours on and the roses will stay fresh longer. However, do remove any leaves that would be submerged in the water. If immersed, they decay rapidly, with unpleasant results for the flower, as well as for your eyes and nose.

I cannot imagine anything more satisfying than creating a vibrant cutting garden. Outdoors the flowers are a visual delight adding color, form, texture, and visual rhythm to a landscape. And indoors, either fresh or dried, they create an instant greeting, bidding welcome to all.

"The Earth laughs in flowers"
—RALPH WALDO EMERSON

THE MAD HATTER

THE INVITATION read: "*HATS—FUN, FABULOUS or FUNKY*" and I immediately thought of one of my favorites, a simple go-to-church straw hat that sat in quiet retirement on a shelf in the closet.

Swathed in yards of tulle loosely stitched to its crown and studded with freeze-dried, hot-glued roses and peonies, my Plain Jane hat was about to embark on a new life. I made my way through my friend's Mad Hatter's Tea Party, crowned with my new creation, and was greeted with delighted oohs and aahs.

Try your hand at decorating a hat even if it's not something you would ever put on your head. A cheery chapeau festooned with garden finds will add charm to a room simply by sitting on a chair. A little imagination can turn an inexpensive straw skimmer into a festive floral centerpiece or a witty alternative to a wreath.

PIECE OF CAKE

A LAYERED FUDGE cake with frothy icing sounds tempting, but temptation soon dwindles when you remember that it will be followed by an hour on the treadmill. Instead, I whip up floral confections that are a feast for the eyes—and free of consequences for the waistline.

Making one of these fanciful, easy-dieter cakes is simple with this no-fail recipe—the list of ingredients is left to the imagination of the baker and can be adapted to suit any occasion. (Just be sure to use blossoms of uniform size.) Serve the finished confection as a gift or keep it for a whimsical display in your kitchen.

"Recipe"

❧ Assorted dried flowers: globe amaranth or strawflowers; rose petals and rosebuds, hydrangea, cockscomb, or gardenia; bay or eucalyptus leaves; seed pods

❧ 1 or 2 pieces of round or wedge-shaped Styrofoam or Floral Foam

❧ Hot glue gun and glue sticks

Cut foam to size. (I stacked two triangles of 2-inch- (5-cm-) thick foam to make a slice that is 4 inches (10cm) high, 6 inches (15cm) wide and about 7 inches (18cm) long. Organize flowers by color and size; practice different arrangements before gluing. When you are satisfied, apply a spot of hot glue to the foam, press a blossom in place, and hold until set. Repeat until the cake is done.

Celebrate a friend's birthday with a piece of cake almost good enough to eat. For Flag Day or Independence Day, I like to make a spectacular red, white, and blue slice.

GARDEN PARTY

ELEBRATING the glory days of summer with a party in the garden is an annual tradition at our Connecticut home. Suddenly no special occasion is needed to entertain except to delight in the natural beauty of the season. Beyond food and drink, it's the sharing of life's unadorned pleasures with family and friends we cherish. There is utmost joy in nonorchestrated simplicity—the riches of nature, simply prepared food, herbs and flowers that nurture a sense of well-being and contentment. Whether you choose a casual picnic or set the table with linens and silver, a summer garden is always the perfect backdrop for your gathering.

Chicken Salad Canapés

3 cups (420g) chopped cooked chicken

2 tablespoons (10g) chopped watercress

2/3 cup (165ml) mayonnaise

1/2 teaspoon curry powder

1/2 cup (60g) chopped walnuts

28 slices premium-quality white bread

Edible flowers

2 1/2" (64cm) biscuit cutter

Combine first five ingredients, mix well and refrigerate until ready to use. With biscuit cutter, cut bread slices into rounds. Place chicken salad mixture on top of bread round. Garnish with additional watercress sprigs and edible flowers. Yield: 28 canapés.

Rose Sugar

Alternate layers of partially dried rose-scented geranium leaves and sugar in a clean glass jar. Cover the jar and set it aside for several days in a cool dry place until the sugar absorbs the essence of rose fragrance. Remove the leaves before serving the sugar.

Floral ice cubes

Add water to ice cube trays until they are half full. Place a small edible flower in each cube. Freeze until firm. Then fill the trays with water completely and freeze them again. (Freezing in two stages keeps the flowers centered.)

Edible flowers

Be sure to use only those that are not toxic and are pesticide-and herbicide-free.

Calendula
Chive blossoms
Dianthus
Hollyhock
Johnny-jump-up
Lavender blossoms
Nasturtium
Pansies
Rose petals
Violet
Zucchini blossoms

GARDEN ROSE WATER

WHAT BETTER way to celebrate the glorious month of the rose than by capturing its magical scent for year-round use? Natural scents soothe our spirits, reminding us of gentler times when life moved at a slower pace and simple handmade gifts brought comfort and pleasure.

I give this floral water in lovely etched bottles decorated with a single dried rose, satin ribbons, and sprigs of baby's breath. A gift card that includes a list of ingredients, suggested usage, and a thoughtful expression never fails to bring a smile of appreciation.

Preparation

Rose water will refresh your spirits and soothe your body. Dab generously at pulse points; sprinkle over bed and bath linens.

1/4 cup (60 ml) vodka

12 drops essential rose oil (available at druggist or health food stores)

2 cups (470 ml) distilled water

1 cup (10 mg) pink or red rose petals

Mix vodka and rose oil in a glass container. Add the water and rose petals. Pour the mixture into spotless bottles and let them stand up to three days in a warm sunny spot. Strain petals from the water and decant mixture into decorative gift bottles. (Not a culinary preparation, do not use internally.) Yield: approximately 2 cups.

"In the garden mystery glows the secret is hidden in the rose."

—FARID UD-DIN ATTAR

July

THE HYDRANGEA

ONG AFTER the petals of my spring-flowering shrubs have faded, my hydrangeas begin to bloom and fill the garden with billowy blossoms of sky blue, rosy pink, and creamy white. This old-fashioned plant with branches laden with voluptuous blossoms graces many summer gardens where it produces armfuls of flowers. Hydrangeas lend an air of gentility to a garden, and their long-blooming flowers also provide spectacular color throughout all the hot days of summer.

The name *hydrangea* is derived from the Greek words for water (*hydro*) and bowl or vessel (*angeion*). But my first hydrangea made me think of another word derived from Greek: chameleon.

A friend in the fashion industry gave me my first hydrangea. She had selected a specific plant because its glorious color recalled a particularly shocking pink that we had discovered on a trip to Paris. But imagine my shock next season when my hot pink plant produced blooms of heavenly blue. After some research I discovered that this striking metamorphosis

was not due to hocus-pocus but to a chemical interaction between the soil and the plant. Acidic soil encourages the hydrangea to absorb aluminum which accounts for the blueness. When the soil is more alkaline, aluminum absorption is prevented, and pink blooms abound. Mopheads—the type my friend had given me—are the least stable of the hydrangeas and most readily change color according to the pH of the soil.

Thus enlightened, my shock gave way to delight, and hydrangeas have since become a stalwart of my garden. Their luxurious blossoms are quite hardy—I leave some on the bush through the winter to hold an echo of summer through the year. The cut

flowers respond well to drying, and add texture and richness to arrangements and wreaths. At Christmas, they make attractive and unexpected ornaments on the tree.

There are more than 500 hydrangea cultivars including various climbers and shrubs with diverse foliage and flowers. With so many elegant choices, you are sure to find a botanical chameleon of your own to enhance your garden with its extravagant blooms, air of old-fashioned gentility, and chromatic magic.

Planting Tips

Lush shrubs of macrophylla hydrangea with abundant blooms are easy to grow.

Happiest in morning sun but will also flower abundantly in light shade.

Will thrive in almost any well-drained soil.

To manipulate color, remember that deep blue results from acidic soil (pH between 4.0 and 5.5) and rich pink from alkaline (7.3 to 7.5). Increase alkalinity with cautious additions of lime. Increase acidity with peat moss, aluminum sulfate, or sulfur. (Pee gee hydrangea slowly turn from white to soft pink to rusty bronze, irrespective of the soil's pH.)

CLIMBERS

VINE IS a free spirit that adds a magical, lyrical quality to all it embraces. Some are treasured for their showy blooms and lush foliage, others for their sweet fragrance or succulent fruit.

My grandfather's grape arbor was a magical place for my sister and me. Nonno's vines spanned over 100 feet and ran the entire length of his garden. He grew grapes to make wine. We thought he grew them for us. We visited every Saturday, and while the adults took a restorative walk after a very hearty lunch, my sister and I sought out the clusters of rich fruit that hung like jewels from the vines above us. Our nimble fingers darted upward, greedily plucking as many grapes as our small hands could hold.

Annual and perennial climbers offer many rewards in the garden. They add a touch of romance, create privacy, enliven small areas, and complement architectural details—all without taking up valuable space. Vines may be deciduous or evergreen, herbaceous or woody, sun- or shade-loving; and may offer flowers, foliage, or fruit. Annual vines are inexpensive, easy to grow, and fast to climb. Perennials produce spectacular color and textural interest year after year.

The appreciation of vines that I learned from my grandfather continues in my own garden. Our stone house is softly draped with Chinese wisteria. In spring it blooms profusely with clusters of amethyst flowers that remind me of Nonno's grapes. Our age-worn fence is cloaked in the majestic purple flowers of *Clematis x jackmanii*. And because our clematis has its feet in the shade and its head in the sun, we are rewarded with a riot of blooms from spring into summer. 'Heavenly Blue' morning glories festoon the lamppost on our front walk annually. A perennial evergreen English ivy cools the porch in summer and screens us from passers-by; in winter it obligingly softens harsh, nor'easterly winter winds.

Find the vines that answer your desires. What could be more romantic than roses cascading over an arbor? or as delicious as masses of honeysuckle rambling over a picket fence? or as delightfully unexpected as colorful nasturtiums scampering through the vegetables? You won't lack choices in this enchanting world.

"Every vine climbing and blossoming tells of love and joy."
—ROBERT G. INGERSOLL

COOL CUCUMBERS

MY TASTE IN cucumbers is slightly experimental. In addition to such popular kinds as gherkins, pickling, and burpless, I enjoy planting heirloom varieties, for example, lemon cucumbers. Their pale yellow color and oval shape add interest to both the garden and the salad bowl. My Dad is more of a traditionalist. He grows only the slicing type, picks them slightly immature to ensure crispness, and enjoys them sliced and dressed simply—just a dash of salt, a sprinkle of wine vinegar, and a drizzle of virgin olive oil.

Whatever your preference, all cucumber plants require consistent moisture and warmth over the growing season if they are to yield a sweet and plentiful harvest. Cucumbers flourish when surrounded by nourishing friends—peas, beans, and carrots. Interplanting can also help maintain a healthy crop: radishes repel beetles, corn helps to prevent the virus that causes wilt, and sunflowers are perfect beach umbrellas for cucumbers varieties that thrive in light shade. Cucumbers have a distinct dislike for potatoes which are subject to phytophthora blight. And please, do remember to keep aromatic herbs, such as sage, at least an arm's length from the cucumber patch—more if space permits.

Cucumber vines may sprawl as far as 6 to 8 feet. The harvest is more plentiful and the plants occupy less space if they have an upright support, so I give my cucumbers a tepee to meander upon. A trellis or tepee adds charm to the garden scene and has the added benefit of keeping the fruit off the ground, which reduces opportunities for fungus.

Plant List

🍀 Hybrid slicers include 'Slice King,' 'Sweet Slice' and 'Sweet Delight'—all are "burpless" and well-suited for salads or snacks.

🍀 Picklers include 'Hybrid Lucky Strike,' which grows on compact vines, and 'Vert de Massy' which are made into cornichons, the little pickles that accompany patés.

🍀 My favorite heirlooms are the round, yellow Lemon cucumbers and the white De Bouenil. The Lemon's mild flavor and crispy texture make them the perfect snack for a thirsty gardener. The De Bouenils are a versatile base for colorful relishes.

FLORAL FRAME

HE SIGN read "Something for everyone," so I turned the car around and headed back to the old Victorian house on the hill. Once there, I passed by the house with its wonderful gingerbread trim, slightly fading paint, and genteel porch and headed for the garage which seemed to be bursting with an odd assortment of intriguing junk.

I picked my way through the dark, dank garage, taking care not to trip on the rusting bed frames, clusters of garden tools, and "as is" power mowers until I spotted an old painted bench in a corner and the wooden frame casually propped up against it. The frame was exactly what I had in mind—it was just the right size and shape and it was perfectly plain. Almost miraculously, it was not warped from the dampness. I walked out into the blinding sun, read the price tag—75 cents—and smiled gleefully. Another "find." The sign had certainly been propitious for me! I couldn't wait to get home and start my frame's "make-over."

P.S. I also bought the painted bench in the corner. (See page 70.)

Materials

Choose a frame with relatively flat surfaces and flowers that complement the colors in the print or photograph that will occupy the finished frame.

🌷 Any size wood frame

🌷 Sheet moss, sufficient to cover the frame

🌷 Hot glue gun and glue sticks

🌷 Craft stick

🌷 A variety of freeze-dried flowers: cockscomb, feverfew, goldenrod, hydrangea, pansy, pincushion flower, Queen Anne's lace, sunflower, viola, zinnia

🌷 Assorted greenery: magnolia leaves, plumosa ferns, lemon leaves

Draw generous beads of glue over the frame. Use the stick to press sheet moss onto the adhesive until the front is covered. Trim straggly pieces. Arrange the flowers and greenery around the frame. Don't glue them down until you have a pleasing arrangement. I placed the larger flowers in the four corners as focal points and clustered the smaller ones for a more delicate balance.

PASTA AL FRESCO

VERYONE LOVES a picnic, no one more than I. When I was growing up, our family often took day trips designed to educate while entertaining. Perhaps we'd go to a re-created Colonial village or to a New England green for a summer festival. But for me, the destination was secondary to the journey because traveling meant a picnic at some wonderful spot along the route. We'd feast on just-picked fruits and vegetables acquired at a roadside stand or farmer's market. The tomatoes were tastier, the cucumbers crunchier, and the peaches sweeter when we ate them under a canopy of leaves and radiant blue sky.

I still delight in outdoor dining. Picnics are a celebration of summer, a time to savor all of the best that the season has to offer. Colorful, simple-to-prepare pastas made with ripe, off-the-vine vegetables are favorites with friends and family alike.

"Bread feeds the body indeed, but flowers feed also the soul."

—THE KORAN

Pasta with Eggplant & Bell Peppers

1 pound (450g) fusilli or other spiral shaped pasta, cooked al dente

1/4 (60ml) cup olive oil

1 large onion, peeled and chopped

4 medium-size bell peppers, 2 red and 2 yellow, stemmed, seeded, and chopped

1 medium-size eggplant, unpeeled, seeded, and cut into 3/4-inch (2cm) cubes

3 large cloves garlic, peeled and chopped

1/2 cup (30g) fresh basil, chopped

1/2 cup (30g) fresh Italian parsley, chopped

1 cup (250ml) vegetable broth

Salt and pepper

3/4 cup (100g) grated Parmesan cheese

1/2 cup (60g) toasted pine nuts, chopped

Heat olive oil in a large heavy skillet for 1 minute. Add onions and cook at medium heat until translucent, but not brown. Add peppers, eggplant and garlic, cook for 10 minutes, stirring occasionally, until peppers soften. Add basil, parsley, and vegetable broth. Simmer, stirring occasionally, until eggplant is tender. Meanwhile, cook pasta for about 12 minutes, drain and set aside in a serving bowl. Remove eggplant mixture from heat, add it to the cooked pasta and toss until the pasta is coated. Season to taste with Parmesan cheese, salt and pepper. Garnish with pine nuts. Serves 6.

MINTY YOGURT CLEANSER

AS A HOME gardener, I am constantly exposed to sun, wind, and heat—all of which are hard on my skin. Fortunately, I am also constantly finding earth-friendly remedies to make from the herbs, fruits, and vegetables that I grow. This easy-to-prepare cleanser is one of my favorite soap substitutes. The mint is deliciously scented and imparts a refreshing coolness to my skin. Yogurt is a mild astringent, and the milk imparts silky softness.

Preparation

This cleanser will keep for several days in the refrigerator.

1/4 cup (60ml) whole milk

3/4 cup (180ml) plain yogurt

2 tablespoons mint, washed and chopped

Cheesecloth

Mix all the ingredients in a blender. Cover and place in the refrigerator for approximately 12 hours. Strain through cheesecloth into a clean bowl or jar. Using a cotton ball, gently apply to face, avoiding the area around the eyes. Rinse with splashes of cool water and moisturize. Yield: about 1 cup

This homemade yogurt cleanser leaves my skin radiant. But before using any homemade preparation, test for allergic reactions. Apply a bit of the preparation to your inner forearm. Cover with an adhesive bandage for up to 24 hours. If a rash or redness appears, do not use the preparation.

August

THE **TOMATO**

ONE TASTE OF a vine-ripened, fresh-from-the-garden tomato and there can be no doubt that the tomato is king. But it was not always so. Early settlers in North America believed this fruit was quite deadly. Folklore suggests that this fear arose because botanists identified the tomato as part of the nightshade family. Since some members of this plant family are poisonous, the assumption was made that the tomato would also be harmful if consumed. So the plant was grown for its ornamental value.

In the Old World, however, people had no such illusions. Europeans' infatuation with the tomato dates back to the 16th century, when Spanish conquistadors brought it home as an example of Mexico's riches. The Italians were the first to exploit the culinary value of this most delicious discovery. Because of its resemblance to the human heart, the ever-romantic French thought the luscious red fruit was an aphrodisiac and dubbed it *pomme d' amour,* the "apple of love."

Americans finally succumbed to the tomato's allure in the 1820s when

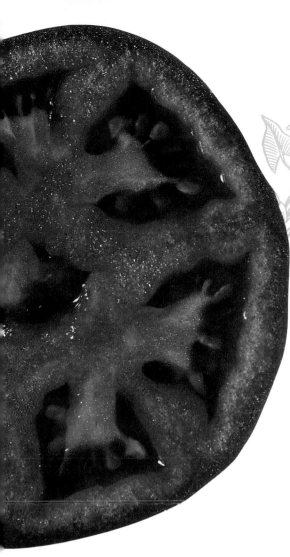

Planting Tips

🍃 Bright light, at least 6 hours of full sun daily. Food. Add nitrogen fertilizer sparingly during early growth, too much will encourage foliage at the expense of flower and fruit development.

🍃 Tomatoes require a good supply of calcium to avoid blossom-end rot, a dark rotting patch on the fruit's bottom. Scattering a handful of finely ground eggshells around the plant will correct the problem.

🍃 Water plants regularly and deeply. Mulch well, especially in hot weather, to avoid cracking.

🍃 Disease prevention. To reduce the chance of disease, avoid planting your tomatoes where you grew them the previous year.

🍃 Tomato cultivars are labeled for disease resistance. Look for varieties with combinations of the letters V (*verticillium wilt*), F (*fusarium wilt*), T (*tobacco mosaic*), N (*nematodes*), and A (*alternaria*) after their names.

🍃 Pest prevention. Interplant nasturtiums, marigolds, parsley, and basil.

🍃 High-density planting may increase production.

Col. Robert Gibbon Johnson successfully consumed a basket of tomatoes on the courthouse steps in Salem, New Jersey. He accomplished this brave feat amidst a carnival-like scene with bands playing and with his physician at his side—just in case! Word of his survival spread quickly and by the mid-1800s farmers and home gardeners alike were enamored of this most savory edible.

"Nature never did betray
the heart that loved her,
tis her privilege through all
the scenes of this our life
to lead from joy to joy."
—WILLIAM
WORDSWORTH

AUTUMN COLOR

WHEN SUMMER'S grand finale begins, I start looking forward to the opening of the fall season, and my garden starts providing cues for the dramatic changes that will occur over the next several weeks. As the days grow shorter and the nights cooler, annuals and summer-blooming perennials step aside and let hardy, vibrant, between-season bloomers take center stage. Butterflies and bumblebees, supporting players to many of these beauties, add enchantment to the scene.

Summer stock ingénues that will blossom into vivid autumn stars include salvia, helenium, goldenrod, black-eyed Susans (in particular, *Rudbeckia fulgida* 'Goldsturm'), and *Aster x frikartii* 'Monch.' Scene-stealing dahlias come in an array of shapes—pompon, cactus, and daisy—and exuberant, bright, brassy colors. Some yield prodigious blossoms that rival the show put on by my mophead hydrangeas. Chrysanthemums, the grande dames of the autumn garden, are valued for their wide range of color, size, and shape.

A perennial headliner in many late season gardens, 'Autumn Joy' sedum has broad clustered flowers that open with a blush of deep pink and gradu-

ally deepen to a warm, rich russet. Hybrid asters, especially 'New York' (*A. novi belgii*) and 'New England' (*A. novae-angliae*), are stalwart fall troupers that offer a profusion of blooms from early autumn through frost when good drainage is provided.

"To everything there is a season, and a time for every purpose under heaven."
—Eccleslastes 3:1

Your autumn garden needn't be all show-stopping color. Frost-tolerant colchicum and autumn crocus are a happy late-season surprise and come in a spectrum of cool colors from lavender to rose. Japanese anemone's delicate flowers bloom in springtime pastels. Ornamental grasses, such as maiden grass, *Miscanthus sinensis*, and fountain grass, *Pennisetum*, add movement to the fall scene.

Many fall-blooming perennials can be purchased in containers and either planted outdoors until the ground freezes or maintained in pots. (Keep track of the plant's care labels, in colder climates some of these beauties will need to overwinter in a shed or garage.) To heighten the drama, I buy late bloomers by the bunch and plant them in masses, keeping the softer pale colors separate from the warmer hues. And I keep several pots of flowers near the front door to say "Warm Welcome" to all.

Audition some autumn bloomers. I'm sure you'll find some steady performers that will give your garden richness and extend its engagement for a few extra months.

COOL-WEATHER HARVEST

LL SUMMER long I have watched bees buzzing through my garden, gathering pollen to make the honey that will see them through the winter. Their industry inspired me to extend my garden's bounty as long as possible. The challenge was to find a way to shelter plants from autumn's capricious coastal storms and the sometimes fierce Connecticut winter. The solution? My husband and I built a cold frame.

A cold frame is simply an earth-filled, bottomless wooden box with a slanted glass or plastic lid that serves as a miniature greenhouse. We built ours with 2 x 8 planks, two old windows, a handful of nails, and some hinges. The windows serve as the lids

and we use two notched sticks to support them at different angles for maximum control of temperature, air flow, and humidity.

The temperature inside the frame ranges from 45°F at night to 75°F during the day (7°C to 24°C). These balmy temperatures let me extend the growing season of herbs, vegetables, and greens through the fall and into the winter. Throughout spring and summer, I use the frame to harden off seedlings that I have started indoors and to start seeds for successive plantings.

If starting seeds for cool weather vegetables in a cold frame or in the garden, plant them a little deeper than usual. Add compost and a 5-10-5 fertilizer to ensure a good supply of nutrients and loosen the soil to improve aeration. Keep the soil moist—a straw mulch will help to retain moisture—until the seeds germinate and keep young plants well-watered. A scattering of lime helps protect broccoli, cabbage, and cauliflower against clubroot.

Plant List

Beets, carrots, chard, collards, kale, endive, leaf lettuce, radishes, spinach, and turnips are among the many delicious, vitamin-rich vegetables that can be started from seed in early August and reach maturity before frigid weather nips them. Check the maturation time when you select vegetable seeds and choose varieties that will mature before the first frost date in your area or that are frost-tolerant. Certain cool-weather vegetables (broccoli, brussels sprouts, cabbage, and cauliflower, in particular) are best planted as transplants at this time of year.

DRYING HERBS

HARVESTING and drying herbs is a pleasure that I yield to with great enthusiasm. The best time to pick herbs is in the morning after the dew has evaporated and before the sun burns off their essential oils. Select herbs that are whole and wholesome, wash them in cold water, and pat them dry with paper towels. Work quickly to preserve as much of the oils as possible.

Hang herbs to dry or arrange a single layer of leaves and flowers on an old screen. Good ventilation speeds the drying process and prevents mold. Store the herbs in airtight glass jars in a dark closet. Date and label them for future reference.

To dry herbs in a microwave oven, arrange the leaves or blossoms on a paper towel. Drying times depend on the kind and quantity of herbs used. Start slow—the herbs may become powdery (or ignite). Begin with 60-second tests, and repeat as needed.

Freeze herbs in labeled plastic bags or containers, or place a teaspoon of a finely chopped herb into an ice cube tray and fill with water. There's no need to defrost the herbs before using them—they can go straight from the freezer into the pot.

To air-dry herbs, tie them in bunches with an elastic band and hang them upside down from a beam, batten, or cord in a warm, dark, dry, well-ventilated place.

SCENTED PILLOW

SCENTED pillows were traditionally used to encourage rest and dreaming. The heady aroma of hop blossoms in particular were thought to induce drowsiness and a relaxed state of mind. Abraham Lincoln, one of America's most burdened presidents, slept surrounded by pillows filled with those flowers.

These small, flat, envelope-shaped pillows are meant to supplement traditional bed pillows, not to replace them. They generally have an inner and outer layer. The inner sack holds the potpourri and is made of a thin, breathable fabric such as muslin or voile with a Velcro closure. It can be removed and refilled with fresh ingredients when the scent fades. The outer shell should be made from a fabric that complements your bedroom and can be decorated with lace, ribbons, buttons, or embroidery.

Choose a soothing combination of herbs and flowers such as lavender, rose petals, lemon balm, chamomile, scented geraniums, or sweet woodruff. Pick through the ingredients and crumble them gently to eliminate prickly sprigs. Add a drop or two of an essential oil to enhance the fragrance, and toss or shake until the ingredients are well-mixed. Store the mixture in an airtight glass container for several days before filling the pillow. Sweet dreams!

"I know a bank where the wild thyme blows, where oxlips and the nodding violet grows... And there sleeps Titania sometime of the night Lull'd in these flowers with dances and delight."

—WILLIAM SHAKESPEARE

HARVEST BOUNTY

 RIED HERBS were sure signs of prosperity in the Middle Ages, when spices came from faraway lands of fantasy and were available only to the wealthy. Today the home gardener has access to a multitude of herbs and can utilize them in a variety of ways. These recipes showcase two formerly exotic ingredients—the tomato and those princely herbs—that have become staples in a cook's garden.

I make the seasoning blends in smallish batches—just enough to last through the winter—because their flavors will start to diminish after 6 to 8 months. Packaged in attractive glass jars tied with lace, fabric, raffia, or ribbon, these healthful flavor enhancers are welcome gifts for family and friends.

Herb Seasonings

Fines Herbes: For egg, fish, and vegetable dishes.

3 tablespoons each of dried tarragon, chervil, parsley, and chives

Yield: about 3/4 cup.

❧

Italian Mix: For pizza, herb bread, or tomato sauces.

1/4 cup each of dried oregano and parsley

1/2 cup dried basil

Yield: about 1 cup.

❧

Herbes de Provence: For stews and grilled poultry and meats.

1/4 cup each dried marjoram and basil

2 tablespoons dried savory

4 tablespoons each dried rosemary and thyme

1 tablespoon dried organic lavender blossoms

1 tablespoon dried fennel seeds

Yield: about 1 cup.

Savory Summer Tarts

1 sheet frozen puff pastry

1–2 tablespoons cold water (to seal dough)

1 cup (115g) shredded cheese: a mixture of mozzarella, Parmesan, and Romano, to taste

2 medium-size plum tomatoes, sliced crosswise

4 heaping tablespoons (50g) grated Parmesan cheese

2 sprigs of fresh basil (garnish)

Preheat oven to 425°F (220°C). With a floured rolling pin, roll out pastry on a lightly floured surface. Cut 2 circles from the pastry by tracing around an 8-inch plate. Brush the edges with water and fold over about 1 inch (2.5cm) to form a wide border. Pleat as needed, sealing surfaces with water. Transfer pizza shells to a large baking sheet. Make a few slits in bottom of pastry so that the shells will bake evenly and hold their shape. Bake for 5 minutes; remove from oven. Divide shredded cheese mix in half and, scatter one half on bottom of each tart. Arrange tomato slices over the cheese. Sprinkle with grated Parmesan. Bake in upper part of oven for 12 to 15 minutes or until cheese has melted and pastry is golden. Garnish with fresh basil. Serve warm or at room temperature. Yield: 2 tarts.

"Summer cooking implies a sense of immediacy, a capacity to capture the essence of the fleeting moment."
—ELIZABETH DAVID

"Acorns
down-pattering
While Autumn
breezes sing."
—JOHN KEATS

AUTUMN

AUTUMN GLORY

UDDENLY UPON us, Autumn is aglow! The brilliant foliage, so deserving of its ardent praise, transforms entire neighborhoods. The cool greens of summer are transformed into opulent drifts of crimson and gold, seemingly painted by a celestial hand. Autumn gardens become miniature landscapes, bejeweled with vivid asters, dahlias, and chrysanthemums. Fall crocuses and colchicums gleam like pearls among the fallen leaves.

In this season of preparation when Nature herself takes the long view, I am most aware of the spiritual aspects of tending a garden. In imitation of nature, I collect seeds for use next spring, tuck bulbs beneath the warm earth in a silent promise of renewal, and cover the garden with a cozy blanket of mulch.

For autumn is a hopeful time, the season of absolute faith. With winter looming, the earth all around us is busily preparing for spring. Where flowers once bloomed, seedpods now burgeon and burst, scattering seeds for the next generation of growth. Succulent berries gently ripen on their vines, becoming rich treasure troves for the feasting birds, which in turn, reward the plants' largess by distributing their seed.

Autumn is also the time of harvest, of feasting and celebration. Window boxes flaunt the royal purple and rich magenta of ornamental cabbages and kale. Checkered Indian corn lends an iridescent shimmer to doorways while jack o' lanterns grin their eerie grins from every portal. Costumed goblins, all in fun, roam from house to house demanding the treats we are happy to give. All the joy of this season, all the gifts of nature form a steady crescendo to Thanksgiving, the traditional feast that celebrates the blessings of family and country, home and hearth.

Leaves rustle underfoot. The sun is lower in the sky, its amber rays coming closer to caress the fall garden. As the days drift by in anticipation of winter, I am at peace, content in the enduring round of the seasons, and completely won over by the majesty of autumn's glory.

"Under the influence of all this loveliness, almost I am persuaded to love autumn best, and forget a lifelong allegiance to the springtime of the year."
—E.V. BOYLE

An Autumn Outing

The cool, bright Fall weather
is an irresistible invitation
to spend time outdoors, and it is
easy to coax me into visiting a pick-
your-own produce farm.
At this time of year, some part
of my mind is always occupied with
plans for the upcoming holidays.
The sight of acres filled with gourds
of every color, shape, and size
always inspires a cartload of
decorating projects. 'Turk's Turban' a
winter squash with a distinctive
rounded bottom topped with a striped
turban makes a rustic centerpiece.
Ornamental gourds, such as the
'Shenot Crown of Thorns' with it's
unusual upright spikes, and the grace-
fully curved, bicolored 'Small Spoon'
create great visual interest in
harvest displays. And the 'warties,'
always in abundance at farm stands,
are irresistible. I invariably start out
shopping with the intention of
buying just one or two of these
goose-bumpy gourds and leave with
an overflowing basket of them.

THINGS TO DO

Early

❧ Pull up spent annuals. Dig up the vegetable garden and clean up the area to prevent harboring pests and diseases through the winter.

❧ Divide perennials that look crowded or are producing fewer flowers.

❧ Sow cool weather vegetables in the garden or cold frame.

❧ Plant peonies, Oriental poppies, and bearded and Japanese irises.

❧ Plant spring bulbs (p.123). At the first hard frost, mulch with 2 to 3 inches (5 to 7cm) of shredded leaves or straw.

❧ Keep a chart of your fall planting for future reference.

Middle

❧ Bring house plants and tender perennials indoors. Check for pests or diseases and treat as needed.

❧ Empty and clean clay pots. Store indoors to prevent cracking.

❧ To extend their harvest time, place a thick layer of salt marsh hay over root crops such as carrots and turnips.

"Gardening is an instrument of grace."
—MAY SARTON

🌿 Mulch evergreens and shallow-rooted plants to protect the root systems. Leave a few inches of bare ground around the base to prevent rot.

🌿 Plant or transplant evergreens, shrubs, and deciduous trees (after leaves fall). Give the new plantings a thorough soaking.

🌿 Drain and store hoses. Drain and turn off outdoor water taps.

🌿 When frost kills foliage on perennials, cut stems to 2 inches (5cm).

🌿 After a heavy frost cut dahlias and gladioli to 1 foot (30cm) from the ground. Dig up the tubers and corms and let them dry out for a few days. Clean them and pack them in boxes with peat moss or sand. Store the boxes in a cool, dry, frost-free place.

🌿 When ground freezes, mound soil about 12 inches (30cm) high at the base of rosebushes. To prevent spreading diseases that may be in the soil, bring in fresh soil; do not scrape soil up from the base of the plant. Place a cylinder of chicken wire around the mound and fill it with loose mulch, such as salt hay or dry leaves.

Late

🌿 Plant tulip and lily bulbs.

🌿 For the best flavor, harvest winter vegetables after the first killing frost.

🌿 When temperature is above 40°F (15°C) spray fine-needled evergreens, rhododenrons, azaleas, and mountain laurels with antidesiccant.

🌿 Drain water from birdbath to avoid freezing and cracking.

🌿 Erect burlap screens around shrubs and young trees to protect from snow, wind, and animals.

Ongoing

🌿 Hang and stock bird feeders and suet racks. Establish a water station.

🌿 Rake fallen leaves. Use some as mulch, compost the rest.

🌿 Take the dog for a long walk.

THE GARDEN HABITAT

THERE ARE very few backyard critters that evoke stronger emotions than squirrels. Their antics can both delight and infuriate the conscientious conservationist. My husband, Michael, has a deep fondness for birds and our garden is well-supplied with feeders and houses that he has made for them. However, our ever-acrobatic squirrels made a sport of scurrying up our century-old hickory tree and leaping from limb to limb to—feeder.

Michael was determined to discourage these furry freeloaders from gobbling the treats intended for winged visitors. He dedicated considerable ingenuity to building a series of squirrelproof feeders that the resourceful rodents just as ingeniously outsmarted. Finally, he devised a feeder that worked. The squirrels were completely repelled by it. Unfortunately, so were most humans, for the once-charming feeder now bristled with metal baffles, spines,

and spokes that pointed every which way. Bowed but unbroken, we took a different tack and replaced the armored feeder with one so larded with appealing treats—corncobs, peanuts, and sunflower seeds—that the sated bandits have abandoned their thieving ways. Sweet peace now reigns between man and beast.

Adventures with marauding mammals notwithstanding, autumn is an especially important time to establish feeders and water stations in the garden. Migrating birds will stop for snacks on their journey south, and natives will learn, early in the season, about a food source and water supply they can depend on. In addition to stocking feeders, we have planted bird-friendly shrubs, trees, and vines in our garden to create an enticing and supportive gathering place for our favorite flocks.

There is a special joy in sharing the garden with birds. By making this space a sanctuary for our feathered visitors, we are rewarded with melodious sounds, eye-catching color, and enchanting motion.

"My only desire is
an intimate infusion with Nature,
and the only fate I wish
is to have worked and lived
in harmony with her laws."
—CLAUDE MONET

September

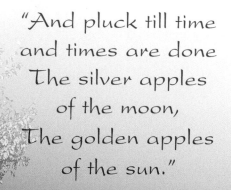

"And pluck till time
and times are done
The silver apples
of the moon,
The golden apples
of the sun."

—WILLIAM BUTLER
YEATS

THE APPLE

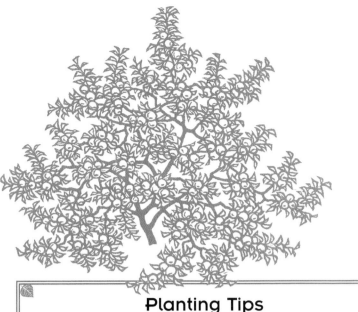

 PPLES ALL about us signal the arrival of autumn. Orchards and backyard trees burst forth with an abundance of ripe favorites. Low-hanging branches are laden with ruby red apples or with russets, golds, greens, and yellows, and resemble Christmas trees bright with glittering ornaments. Each different type beckons; each variety tempts with its characteristic virtues. As an apple lover, I want to spread the good news about heirloom apples. With more markets offering these old-time delights, we can now taste fruits identical to those that sustained and delighted our ancestors in the Old World.

Apples are not native to the Americas. Wild apples grew along the ancient Silk Route that wound from China to eastern Europe through India, Persia, and Turkey. As traders traveled this highway, they collected apple seeds and brought them to Europe for cultivation. In time, colonists carried apple seeds to the New World. In the 18th century, Thomas Jefferson and George Washington helped popularize apples. Avid pomologists, they established orchards at Monticello and Mount Vernon to propagate new varieties.

Many apple varieties vanished and others were superseded by varieties that were developed to meet certain requirements, such as beauty or long storage time. Although more disease-resistant, these commercial varieties offer limited taste, aroma, and texture. Fortunately, many smaller growers have revived the delectable heirlooms and brought them to market.

Planting Tips

🍃 Ideal soil is well-drained with a pH range of slightly acid to neutral (6.0 to 7.0).

🍃 Plant in a sunny location, preferably on a slight slope to avoid the blossom-killing frost that may occur at the bottom of a hill.

🍃 Provide adequate amounts of potassium and calcium to young apple trees.

🍃 Interplant two or more varieties to ensure cross pollination and fruiting. A few varieties—Golden Delicious and Rome Beauty, for example—are self-pollinating.

🍃 Water regularly.

🍃 Prune annually in late winter to encourage growth.

🍃 Keep the ground around the trees free from debris. Remove dead branches and rotting leaves which may harbor harmful fungi spores.

🍃 Do not plant near junipers; they are an alternate host for a fungus called cedar apple rust.

ORNAMENTAL TREES & SHRUBS

 HE NEW ENGLAND seasons offer an ever-changing land- scape, and autumn holds a special magic. The native trees and shrubs put forth such a dazzling display of color that at times I feel I have to catch my breath. The fall foliage that ignites the countryside can warm your own garden as well.

I remember when my husband and I saw our present home for the first time. It was a glorious October day, and the cozy Connecticut neighbor- hood nestled against Long Island Sound was alive with color. We pulled into the driveway, and a magnificent Japanese maple tree, its sinuous branches radiant with fiery red leaves, welcomed us to the home we were about to fall in love with.

As we settled in and I began devel- oping the garden, I added shrubs to enliven our home's winter landscape and help to nourish birds and other wildlife through the season of cold. In particular, I planted a firethorn (*Pyracantha*), and trained it to grow along our rustic back fence. Firethorn is a year-round garden bonanza. It

has fragrant white flowers from early in the growing season into summer. From late summer until winter its stems burgeon with brilliant clusters of vermilion berries. In winter, its 'blooms' are the living blossoms of hungry flocks feasting on the berries.

Trees and shrubs provide perma- nence and strong architectural inter- est to a home garden. Plant them where they can be enjoyed and admired by you and by your neigh- bors. Stake them until they become established, water deeply, and apply fertile top-dressings, and they will reward you through the years with their various seasons of delight.

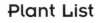

Plant List

❧ The genus Viburnum includes shrubs with strong spring and fall interest. Both the American and European cranberry bush *(V. trilobum and V. opulus)* yield red fruit that remain into late winter.

❧ The autumn foliage colors and vivid red berries of the Japanese Barberry *(Berberis thunbergii)*, enliven late-season landscapes as does winterberry *(Ilex verticillata)*, a native deciduous holly. Northern Bayberry *(Myrica pensylvanica)* produces the fragrant fruits prized by candlemakers.

❧ Red or yellow twig dogwood *(Cornus alba, C. stolonifera)*, add welcome splashes of color. The dramatically twisted branches of Harry Lauder's walking stick *(Corylus avellana 'Contorta')* are a living sculpture in the winter garden. In deepest February, the bright yellow flowers that spangle the stark branches of a Witch Hazel shrub *(Hamamelis spp.)* will warm your heart.

❧ Scale is important when choosing trees, so consider the tree's mature size before planting. Some that are useful in home landscapes are: white birch *(Betula)*, European and Korean mountain ash, hawthorns *(Crataegus)*, red Maple *(Acer rubrum)*, and Bradford pear.

Euonymous (top) is also called burning bush. Rosa rugosa (above) produces nutritious fruits. Purple Beautyberry (right) adds a cool note to autumn's fire.

PRESERVING FLOWERS

Screen drying, a variation of air-drying, is used for flowers with large or flat blossoms, such as yarrows or sunflowers.

Y PULSE quickens when I am in the garden selecting flowers to dry. I gather them mid morning on warm sunny days when the sun has dried the dew but not parched the blooms and I pick those that are still slightly budded or only just fully open. While working, my eager mind is busy picturing all the dramatic arrangements I can create and planning potpourris rich with the lush scents of summer.

Three of the easiest preservation methods are: air-drying, water-drying (which works by evaporation), and using a medium such as glycerin or borax. Some are better suited to certain flowers, and some work better for large quantities. Moist and dry media are not recommended for culinary plants.

Air-dry flowers the same way that you air-dry herbs (p.96): strip excess foliage from the stems and hang them upside down in a warm, dark, dry, airy room. The flowers can be hung individually or in bunches. If you bunch them, secure the bunches with rubber bands; the bands will contract as the stems shrink. Most flowers will take about three weeks to air-dry.

Water-drying is a slower process, but billowy flowers such as hydrangea respond best to this method. Stand the flowers in a vase in a few inches of water. The flowers will dry gradually as the water evaporates and retain their plump, natural forms.

Drying media, or desiccants, are best suited for flowers with delicate or multiple petals. Silica gel, sand, and borax are popular desiccants. When using desiccants, place 1 inch (2cm) of the medium in a box, carefully place the flowers in it, sprinkle more medium over them, and cover the box. Leave it for a few days while the moisture is drawn from the plant.

Glycerin, a moist medium, is used to keep leafy branches supple. The process is similar to water-drying: mix 1 part glycerin with 2 parts hot water in a vase, strip foliage from the end of the branch, crush the end with a hammer, and set it in the mixture. As it is absorbed, the glycerin replaces the water in the branch. (The color of the leaves and branch usually alters.) The process is complete when the foliage is supple and slightly glossy.

Preserved flowers bring vibrancy to my home with their dramatic colors and diverse textures. When the cold rain and harsh winds of a nor'easter blow outside my window, a glance at my dried-flower bouquets is all it takes to remind me of the garden they came from and to trigger dreams of spring.

Plant List

🦋 Plants suitable for air-drying include amaranthus, artemisia, astilbe, bachelor button, cockscomb, delphinium, German statice, globe amaranth, globe thistle, goldenrod, lady's mantle, larkspur, liatris, and yarrow.

🦋 Use the desiccant method for flowers with complex or fragile blossoms such as calendula, coreopsis, dahlia, marigold, peony, rose, snapdragon, and zinnia.

🦋 Use the glycerin method for leaves of shrubs, trees, and vines such as beech, boxwood, crab apple, ivy, magnolia, oak, red maple, and viburnum.

🦋 Water drying is the best choice for baby's breath, bells of Ireland, and hydrangea.

HARVEST WREATH

OMPOSED OF natural objects that reflect the changing seasons, a wreath is a versatile decoration with an ancient heritage. Early agrarian societies offered wreaths to the gods to secure future crops. Bursting with nature's bounty, this bold beauty echoes that tradition. Its vibrant colors and textural variety are a celebration of a fruitful harvest.

Whether a wreath is simple or elaborate, square or round, small or large, sacred or mundane, it serves as a reminder of the earth's manifold goodness. Hang one on a door, in a window, over a mantle—anywhere!

Materials

🌺 Grapevine or straw wreath base

🌺 Florist's wire or nylon fishing line

🌺 Florist's picks

🌺 Hot-glue gun and glue sticks, as needed

🌺 Assorted decorations: preserved oak leaves and wisps of wheat, dried herbs and flowers, dried fruits and vegetables, mini gourds, nuts, seedpods, and pine cones

Secure a loop of wire or fishing line to the base to form a hanger. Glue preserved oak leaves to the base, working in one direction or out from the center. Hide stems beneath adjacent leaves. Tie herbs and flowers into bundles with florist's wire or fishing line. Attach bundles to the base with hot glue, wire, or fishing line, or tie them to florist's picks and push the picks into the base. Use picks for heavy or bulky items, such as pine cones or dried vegetables. Fill in bare spots with additional bundles or leaves. Hide stems, picks, and wire under adjacent decorations.

POMANDER

THE TRADITION of using pomanders—mixtures of aromatic substances—to sweeten the air dates back to Elizabethan England. In those days, the pomander was practical as well as pretty. An aristocrat's pomander contained mixtures of fragrant herbs, exotic spices, and costly perfumes that were meant not only to please the nose on crowded streets, but also to protect against the danger of plague and other infections. Commoners could not afford the ingredients in these lavish pomanders. So they were more likely to sport the poor man's pomander: an apple or orange studded with cloves.

Scented pomanders are an imaginative way to sustain the marvels of the outdoors in your home all year round. I keep several rose- or lavender-scented ones in my guest bathroom, and friends often sheepishly confess to peeking around, searching for the source of the lovely scent. During the holidays, I place bowls brimming with spicy citrus pomanders in our front hallway. Their enticing aroma welcomes guests as soon as they step through the door.

Materials

🌿 8 to 10 oranges

🌿 Whole cloves with large heads

🌿 Wooden skewer, nutpick, or slim knitting needle

🌿 Pen (optional, to mark the design)

🌿 Fixative and spice powder: 1/2 c. cinnamon, 1/4 c. powdered cloves, 2 tablespoons each powdered nutmeg, allspice, and orrisroot

Mix the fixative powder in a container large enough to hold the oranges. Mark the design on each orange. Pierce the skin with the skewer, making only a few holes at a time. Push a whole clove into each of the holes. Roll the clove-studded fruit in the fixative powder until it is completely covered. Leave the fruit in the fixative and place the container in a warm dry place for several weeks. Turn the oranges from time to time so that they will dry out evenly.

APPLE DELIGHTS

THE PRODIGIOUS assortment of apples that nature and cultivation have given us inspires equally enormous enjoyment. Whether cooked into pies and cakes, pressed into sauces, cider, or spreads, or simply eaten in all its just-plucked-from-the-tree goodness, the apple has no peer.

Whether you want fruit for snacking, baking, or condiments, this list should be a helpful guide for the apple adventurer that lives inside you.

Eating apples include: 'Baldwin,' 'Fuji,' 'Macoun,' 'Mutsu,' 'Melrose,' and 'Royal Gala.' For baking choose 'Gravenstein,' 'Winesap,' 'Northern Spy,' 'Jonathan,' or 'Newtown Pippin.' Juice and cider lovers fare best with 'Hyslop,' 'Golden Russet,' 'Sops of Wine,' and 'Roxbury Russet.' When making condiments, use 'Idared,' 'Melrose,' or 'Gravenstein' for sauce; and 'Granny Smith,' 'Rhode Island Greening,' or 'Baldwin' for salsa. My favorite for apple butter is the 'Red Royal Limbertwig.'

"Sustain me
with raisins,
Refresh me
with apples."
—SONG OF
SOLOMON 2:5

Apple Salsa

2 large apples (1 baking, 1 green)

1 medium-size garlic clove, chopped fine

1/2 cup (125g) onion, chopped fine

1/2 cup (75g) seedless raisins

1/2 medium-size red pepper, diced

1/4 cup (50g) sugar

1/4 cup (60ml) each of olive oil and cider vinegar

1 tablespoon (15ml) Dijon mustard

Salt and pepper to taste

1/3 cup (20g) flat-leaf parsley, chopped fine

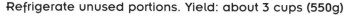

Quarter apples, remove and discard core and seeds. Leaving skin on, chop apples. In a 2-quart (1.9-l) saucepan, combine all the ingredients. Heat to boiling over high heat. Reduce heat to low. Cook, stirring often until apples and onions are tender and liquid has been absorbed (approximately 20 minutes). Set aside to cool. Serve at room temperature. Refrigerate unused portions. Yield: about 3 cups (550g)

Baked Apples with Chestnut Stuffing

3/4 cup (175g) canned chestnuts

6 tablespoons (90ml) maple syrup

1/4 cup (50g) dark brown sugar

1 teaspoon (5ml) ground cinnamon

1/4 teaspoon nutmeg

1/2 cup (120ml) orange and cranberry juice (mixed half and half or to taste)

1/3 cup (50g) seedless raisins

4 baking apples

1 tablespoon (15ml) lemon juice

1 cinnamon stick

Preheat oven to 350°F (180°C). Place chestnuts and their liquid in a saucepan and heat until just below simmering. Remove from heat. Drain chestnuts and puree with 3 tablespoons (45ml) of maple syrup, 3 tablespoons (38ml) of dark brown sugar, 1/2 teaspoon of ground cinnamon, 1/4 teaspoon of nutmeg, and 1/4 cup (60ml) of the juice mixture. Stir in raisins and set aside. Core and seed the apples, making sure to avoid piercing the bottoms. Place apples in a shallow baking dish. Brush inside of apples with lemon juice and sprinkle with remaining cinnamon. Top apples with chestnut mixture. Combine the remaining brown sugar, maple syrup, and juice; pour mixture over the apples. Add the cinnamon stick to the dish and bake, basting occasionally, until apples are tender (approximately 60 minutes). Yield: 4 servings.

INDIAN SUMMER POTPOURRI

ROM ANCIENT to modern times, natural scents have been used to sweeten our homes and soothe our spirits. Today, we still use potpourri for those purposes and a multitude more—to mirror the changing seasons, to celebrate a special holiday, or to enhance the ambiance in a particular room.

There are many ready-made potpourris, but developing a blend that is both original and personal is enjoyable and rewarding. I prefer handcrafted potpourri that is as enticing to the eye as it is to the nose, so I combine the fruits of Mother Nature's beneficence in a way that celebrates the richness of texture and color.

This Indian summer potpourri captures the soul of the season. The warm, robust aroma of apples, cinnamon, and cloves evokes the sensual delights of an excursion to an apple orchard on a glorious fall day.

"Here's flowers for you hot lavender, mints, savory, marjoram, the marigold that goes to bed with the sun"
—WILLIAM SHAKESPEARE

Preparation

2 to 4 tablespoons (30 to 60g) fixative (orrisroot chips)

20 drops cinnamon oil

10 drops clove oil

5 drops apple fragrance oil

1 cup dried lemon geranium, lemon verbena, and/or lemon leaves

1 cup dried apple slices

2 to 3 cups dried berries, flowers, and small pine cones (in any ratio that pleases you)

4 or 5 dried miniature pomegranates

10 or 12 cinnamon sticks (pieces about 3 inches long)

Locking plastic bag or glass jar with lid

Large container with close-fitting lid

Put the fixative and oils in a locking plastic bag or a glass jar with lid. Seal the bag (or tightly cover the jar), shake well, and set it aside for 2 weeks to allow the scents to blend. Combine the remaining ingredients in the large container. Add the scented mixture, cover tightly, and shake to distribute the oil-impregnated fixative. Store the container for an additional week. When the mixture is fully cured, pour it into a decorative basket or bowl and stir the potpourri. Then put a log in the fireplace, settle into a cozy sofa, and enjoy the fragrance of the season.

October

THE PUMPKIN

ALLOWEEN and pumpkins are inseparable. Even now as an adult, I believe that the magic of the season would not be complete without a ritual visit to a pumpkin farm. The day that Michael and I set aside for our journey begins early, and the morning is taken up with a leisurely drive along the country roads of rural Connecticut. October is peak foliage season and we make frequent stops at roadside lookout points to drink in the spectacular kaleidoscope of fiery color. The many stops we make not only remind us why our Northeastern autumns are so celebrated but also heighten our anticipation for the task ahead: selecting our best-ever pumpkin.

Driving down the dusty, well-worn lane to the farm, we are mesmerized by an orange landscape stretching out on either side as far as the eye can see. In the parking lot, I scramble out of the car almost before it stops, and in an instant I'm off to the pumpkin patch. When Michael catches up, we pace up and down the rows. Making our selections takes some time, for there are now many varieties available to tempt pumpkin lovers.

Should we choose a 'Connecticut Field,' a favorite for carving into great big lanterns that light the way for eager trick-or-treaters? Or perhaps a 'Lumina' whose ghostly white skin is the perfect canvas for my paintbrush. Or a ribbed, misty-green 'Jarrahdale' for an exotic touch? Holiday pie-making demands a delicately textured 'Rouge Vif d'Etampes' —the classic model for Cinderella's coach. Armfuls of miniature 'Baby Bear' and 'Jack-Be-Little' pumpkins —for displaying in a cornucopia, to hold dips and relishes, to use as soup bowls or as votives—round out our mission.

Delighted with our selection and ravenous from our expedition, we conclude our visit with a stop at the farm's snack bar for the well-earned refreshment of homemade doughnuts and hot spiced cider—a New Englander's High Tea.

Planting Tips

Pumpkins need a lot of space. Their spreading vines can extend 20 feet or more, so many home gardeners prefer to leave the growing to a farmer.

- Plant in full sun, in rich, well-drained soil.
- Start seeds indoors 3 to 4 weeks before the danger of frost has passed.
- Plant seedlings 3 feet (90cm) apart with rows 4 to 5 feet (120 to 150cm) apart.
- Water thoroughly once a week.
- Pinch off growing tips to control the sprawling vines.

Pumpkins spark our imaginations. When painted, carved, or otherwise embellished, ordinary pumpkins are magically transformed into festive jack-o'-lanterns, scary cats, grinning jesters— even galaxies of stars and moons.

PLANTING SPRING BULBS

"Clean and round, Heavy and sound, Inside every bulb a flower is found."

—OLD POEM

FLOWERING BULBS are the cherished harbingers of spring. How miraculous that such a dazzling display arises from such homely beginnings. A minimal investment of time and money in the fall is rewarded in the spring—and spring after spring—with a spectacular, ever-widening tapestry of color, texture, and fragrance.

In addition to true bulbs (daffodils, tulips, hyacinths, and lilies), this plant category includes corms (crocuses, colchicums, and gladioli), tubers (begonias, anemones, and cyclamens), tuberous roots (dahlias and foxtail lilies), and rhizomes (irises and trilliums). When selecting bulbs, choose those that are big, firm, and plump—generally the bigger the bulb the bigger the bloom. Avoid bulbs that are soft or have moldy spots.

When planting, the trusty adage "Mother Nature knows best" is especially apt, and imitating nature is easier than you might imagine. Choose a spot with rich, sandy, well-drained soil that is easily viewed from your favorite window and plant bulbs in abundance, en masse, and in natural, free-form drifts. Prepare the ground by digging a wide trench and working in compost or leaf mold.

A good rule of thumb is to plant the bulbs three times as deep as they are high. Hold the thought that anything too studied looks artificial—then throw caution to the wind and toss a handful of bulbs up in the air. Plant them, root-end-down, wherever they land. This landscaping "method" is a great stress-buster, and you will be pleased with the results of your no-design-is-the-best-design strategy.

If you are a formalist, use a bulb planter to make 6- to 8-inch (15- to 20-cm) holes for large bulbs, and 2- to 4-inch (5- to 10-cm) holes for smaller bulb species. Space small bulbs 3 to 4 inches (8 to 10cm) apart and large bulbs 5 to 6 inches (14 to 16cm) apart. Topdress with any commercial bulb fertilizer.

With either method, cover the bulbs with top soil and water them thoroughly. In cold zones, bulbs can be left in the ground. In warm and temperate zones (temperatures remain above 20°F/6°C), chill the bulbs in a brown paper bag in the refrigerator (away from fruit) for 8 to 10 weeks before planting.

Select bulbs with different bloom times for a show of color from late winter through summer. Left undisturbed, the bulbs will colonize and produce profusely for years to come.

TWIG CHAIRS

AKE YOUR SEAT, please! Well, not exactly, but these whimsical doll-size chairs are fun to make and add a rustic accent to a shelf or mantel. The materials can be found close to home—just scout your garden or any neighborly glade.

A companionable helper is always a boon to such a scouting mission. Walks with Jake, my gentle Labrador retriever, always yielded a trove of treasures. We found pine cones by the dozen, colorful berries, bittersweet tangled with grapevine, and, of course, sticks, never differentiated by Jake from the shapely twigs scattered about. Refreshed and inspired, we would return home with a bag full of riches, eager for what lay ahead.

Materials

- Assorted slim (1/4-inch/1cm) twigs and branches
- Pruning clippers, sharp utility knife, or small saw
- Hot-glue gun and glue sticks, as needed
- Assorted botanicals: dried flowers, herbs, or grasses; pine cones, nuts, or seedpods; moss

With clippers, cut twigs into short lengths (2 to 4 inches/5 to 8cm). Use one piece as a cross brace. Dab hot glue on the brace and hold a second twig in place until the glue sets. Continue adding twigs to form a chair. Let glue set after each addition. Test the arrangement of the botanicals until you have something pleasing. Remove the decorations, dab the chair with more hot glue and gently press the decorations in place.

FESTIVE CANDLES

A LIT CANDLE creates a magical ambiance. In my parents' generation candles were saved for special occasions— perhaps a party or holiday. Today we light votives, pillars, and tapers as part of our daily routine. I particularly like candles in my kitchen. The warm light from a flickering candle dancing on the wall is guaranteed to lift my spirits on the bleakest of days. And a whiff of the divine fragrance from a scented candle always makes me feel pampered and quite special.

Candles are made even more personal when embellished with everlasting flowers, fragrant herbs, dried fruits, nuts, cones, seed heads or bark. These seasonal botanicals can simply encircle the base of the candle to impart color and textural interest. I placed the pillar (see photo, above) in a nest of grapevine, twigs, and other cuttings from the woods and embellished it with goldenrod, safflower, and bittersweet. The candlestick (left) is draped with pepperberries and ivy sprigs that have been preserved with glycerine.

Using a myriad of dried and fresh botanicals to festoon candles is an elegant and easy method to brighten your home. But, please, *never* leave a candle burning unattended. When the flame is within 3 inches of the decorations, extinguish it and replace the candle.

FALL FARE

OOL DAYS and chilly evenings—weather made to order for soup! Nothing brings a sense of warmth and contentment to the table more than a nourishing bowl of scrumptious homemade soup. And autumn brings with it a cornucopia of vegetables whose rich flavors are enhanced by the long slow cooking that yields savory soup.

A harvest of seasonal fruits and nuts can be combined to make a delectable chunky relish. The autumnal blend of tart cranberries and tangy oranges is a perfect accompaniment for poultry, lamb, or veal. (This relish, however, is so delicious you'll also find yourself eating it by the spoonful.)

Harvest Soup

1 large butternut squash

1/4 cup (60ml) olive oil

1 medium-size onion, chopped fine

2 shallots, minced

2 tablespoons (30ml) garlic, minced

1/2 cup (112g) chopped celery

1 pound (450g) carrots, peeled and chopped

4 cups (950ml) water

1 cup (240ml) chicken broth

1/4 teaspoon nutmeg

Cut squash in half and remove seeds. Cover bottom of a microwave-safe dish with water. Add squash, skin side up, and place in microwave. Cook until flesh is soft, about 15 minutes. Scoop flesh from skin and set aside. In a large saucepan, heat olive oil. When hot but not smoking, lower the temperature, add onions, shallots, and garlic, and cook until soft, but not brown. Add celery, carrots, squash, water, and chicken broth. Bring to a boil. Reduce heat and simmer for about 45 minutes. Add nutmeg. Remove from heat and puree soup in batches in a food processor.
Yield: 4 to 6 servings.

Orange-Cranberry Relish

1 cup (240ml) water

1 cup (200g) sugar

12-ounce (340-g) bag fresh cranberries,
rinsed and patted dry

1/2 cup (75g) raisins

1/4 orange with skin, minced

1/4 lemon with skin, minced

1/2 cup (60g) walnuts, chopped coarsely

Bring water to a boil in a medium-size saucepan.
Add sugar, stir to dissolve. Add cranberries.
Reduce heat. Simmer 10 to 15 minutes, stirring
occasionally. Remove from heat, stir in raisins,
lemon, orange, and walnuts. Set aside to cool
at room temperature. The mixture will thicken
as it cools. Refrigerate any unused portions.
Yield: about 2 1/2 cups (600g).

*"Of soup and love,
the first is best."*

—SPANISH PROVERB

"How could such sweet and wholesome hours Be reckoned but with herbs and flowers?"

—Andrew Marvell

SWEET BAGS & SACHETS

 WEET BAGS and sachets are a delightful way to perpetuate aromatic treasures from the garden. I place these scented sacks throughout the house—selecting fabrics, trims, and fragrances to complement each room. In the dining room, velvet and organza sweet bags exude the scents of lavender, rose, and rosemary—an antique bouquet reminiscent of an English high tea. In the bedroom, an ivory linen pouch filled with calendula and lemon verbena enhances the romantic ambiance. Place sweet bags and sachets anywhere you would like to savor the preserved perfume of a garden.

Preparation

Choose a predominating fragrance or create distinctive mixtures for each room. (If you do not sew, ask the fabric store to recommend a seamstress.)

4 to 6 cups dried mixed botanicals, such as fruit, flowers, herbs, or spices, and fillers such as evergreen twigs and needles, small pine cones, and wood shavings.

1 tablespoon fixative (orrisroot powder or cellulose)

1 teaspoon finely ground cinnamon, clove, nutmeg or allspice (or a blend)

5 to 10 drops of pleasing essential oils, such as bergamot, jasmine, tuberose, or ylang-ylang

Combine the ingredients in a covered glass jar. Shake well to blend and place in a cool, dark place to mellow for about 10 days before filling the sachets.

November

"A thing of beauty is a joy forever."
—JOHN KEATS

THE EVERLASTINGS

HE FLEETING pleasure of a summertime bouquet fades all too quickly, leaving our spirits dampened. As symbols of continuity and undying remembrance, everlasting flowers capture the glory of the high season and lend an ambiance of romance, warmth, and permanence to our fast-paced lives.

In spring and summer, I am mindful of the coming autumn and winter. When planning my summer garden, I always include generous, varied plantings of these sure-to-endure beauties. Then when these long autumn evenings come, I sort through my hoard of preserved treasures, happily composing bouquets and nosegays, filling baskets and vases, and sweetening all with delicious essential oils.

This family of plants offers an endless array of inspiring shapes, colors, and textures. Spiky spheres of globe thistle, papery tangerine-colored Chinese lantern, and silvery honesty sparkle like lights at an elfin ball. The starry shapes and cheery colors of pincushion flower, statice, and lark-spur brighten my home year-round. Cockscomb's velvety magenta is as vibrant in preservation as it was in the garden the day I picked it.

In this throwaway world of disposable commodities, I truly treasure everlastings for their graceful endurance, timeless beauty, and nonchalant versatility. Many everlastings are annuals that grow effortlessly and quickly, and reward repeated cutting with repeated blooming from early summer until the first frost. Keep your garden and your floral storehouse well stocked with annuals such as globe amaranth (*Gomphrena*), plumed and crested forms of cockscomb (*Celosia plumosa, C. cristata*), lacy love-in-a-mist (*Nigella damascena*), orange safflower (*Carthamus tinctorius*), and apple-green bells of Ireland (*Molucella laevis*). Perennial varieties include baby's breath (*Gypsophilia paniculata*), spiny sea holly (*Eryngium*), yarrow (*Achillea millefolium*), sea lavender (*Limonium latifolium*) and Queen Anne's lace (*Daucus carota*).

With so many choices, you may find that your only problem is having enough space to display all the arrangements your creavity yields.

FORCING BULBS

WHEN FEATHERS of frost begin tickling my windows, I know the time has come for forcing bulbs. An extravagant indoor display of flowering plants is the perfect antidote for a gardener's winter blues.

Bulbs are grouped into two categories: hardy and tender. The hardy kinds include: crocuses, daffodils, hyacinths, grape hyacinths, squills (*Scilla* and *Puschkinia*), glory-of-the-snow, snowdrops, iris reticulata, and tulips. Tender bulbs include amaryllis, paperwhites, Easter lily, calla lily, and Star-of-Bethlehem.

For near-instant gratification, start with the tender bulbs. I like to have masses of paperwhites throughout the house. So I nestle crowds of bulbs—shoulder to shoulder and noses up, please!—in decorative bowls. Paperwhites don't need soil, but do scatter pebbles in the bowl to anchor the bulbs, then add water. After a week or two in a cool, dim spot, the bulbs are well rooted and foliage appears. Move the container into a cool, brightly lit spot. Keep the water level just at the base of the bulb to avoid rot. In about three weeks, you will have pots of fragrant flowers to sweeten your day.

With its cluster of vivid, trumpet-like flowers and shapely 2- to 3-foot

stems, the amaryllis (*Hippeastrum*) is unmatched for drama. To coax this beauty into bloom, soak the bulb in lukewarm water for 2 hours, then plant it in a pot slightly larger than the bulb. Fill the pot two-thirds full with potting soil and place in a warm, sunny room. Water sparingly until the bulb starts to show growth, thereafter keep soil evenly moist. Hardy bulbs must experience cold before they will bloom. In warm climates, place the bulbs in a paper bag and put the bag in a refrigerator (away from

fruit) for 8 to 12 weeks. In cold climates, simply pot the bulbs, water them, and place the pots in a dark, cold, frost-free location such as an unheated garage or put them in a cold frame. When the bulbs sprout, bring the pots into a cool, dimly lit spot. After a week or two, bring them into a sunny room to bloom. Stagger your planting times so that you can have a house filled with flowers from December into April. The doldrums of winter will be greatly alleviated— I guarantee it.

"Flowers really do intoxicate me."
—Vita Sackville-West

THANKSGIVING TABLE

NE OF THE greatest joys of gardening is using the glories of the autumn harvest to bedeck your home for Thanksgiving. Creating a festive seasonal atmosphere by bringing the garden inside adds an extra dollop of pleasure to the holiday celebrations. Ideas are as abundant as the season: a treasure chest of multicolored gourds, window swags of preserved leaves in a blaze of tawny fall colors, bittersweet garlands for chandeliers and picture frames. And of course a lavish display of fall fruits and vegetables—ornamental kale and cabbage, winter squash, pumpkins, pears, blood oranges, and grapes—for the table or sideboard.

I will seize any occasion to make artful baskets, bouquets, centerpieces, and place settings. And the Thanksgiving season is one of the happiest such times. The fun begins with a selection of rustic baskets, weather-kissed garden urns, glazed terra-cotta pottery, majolica pitchers, and lush paisley textiles whose rich, sun-soft-

ened, warm-earth colors and textures will form the palette for the holiday table. Next there's the adventure of combining in attractive and unexpected ways the gifts from my garden and the gleanings from my frequent walks. For example, an assortment of seasonal fruit, flora, and foliage makes a dazzling centerpiece. The eclectic mix of mophead and peegee hydrangeas, chili peppers, checkered corn, scented eucalyptus, giant seed-

Welcome guests to the table with "outdoor" place settings. Twig place mats lend a sylvan feel. Use small clay pots filled with moss and topped with dainty lady apples as place card holders. (A twig holds the card.) Twined vines are nests for dried cranberry "eggs."

"Bless our hearts
to hear
in the breaking
of the bread
the song of the
universe."
—Fr. John B.
Giuliani

pods, and vivid bittersweet in the
osier gathering basket (shown, above)
is a rustic yet sophisticated feature in
the holiday décor. A vase overflowing
with goldenrod, sunflowers, weeping
amaranthus, and an arching branch of
persimmon deserves a place of honor.

Give in to the glory of autumn. Let
your imagination roam free as you
prepare to celebrate the fruits of your
summer labors and the rewards of the
harvest season.

MANTEL DECORATION

HE FIRST CHILL in the air finds me as close as I can get to the fireplace in our living room, luxuriating in the radiant warmth and delighting in the flickering play of light. The carved mantel is the room's focal point, and one of my favorite spots for seasonal decoration. If you don't have a mantel in your house, a bookshelf, long table, or deep window ledge can serve handsomely as a stage for your own creativity.

I chose a long birch basket for a rustic cornucopia to showcase an informal display of autumnal finds—tangles of bittersweet, pine cones, papery Chinese lanterns, colorful Indian corn, brilliant leaves, and graceful twigs. Don't overlook the charm of using favorite objects from around your home. My vintage Staffordshire porcelain dogs add interest and style to this still life.

FRAGRANT BASKETS

WHEN YOUR home needs a decorating boost, a fragrant basket is an ideal choice. Simply select a basket whose size, shape, and embellishments will best complement your décor, fill it with a blend of aromatic botanicals that delight the eye and beguile the nose, and place it in a setting where its subtle charm will enchant all who come calling during this festive season.

I like to use dried hydrangea blossoms from my garden. Even this late in the year, I can find some still clinging to their stems. The billowy beige blooms are not only a great filler but also an impeccable backdrop for any natural display. (A mirror is another wonderful backdrop—effortlessly doubling the visual impact of your handiwork.)

> *"Earth fills her lap with pleasures of her own."*
> —WILLIAM WORDSWORTH

Preparation

Basket (with handle)

Hot-glue gun and glue sticks, as needed

Sheet moss or dried ferns, as needed

Dried botanicals: cockscomb, pepperberries, roses, hydrangeas

Tissue paper

Dried rose petals, lavender blossoms

Essential oil (lavender or rose geranium)

Place the basket on a sturdy work surface. Working in sections, run beads of hot glue along the handle and edges of the basket. Press moss or ferns onto the adhesive, being careful to avoid burning your fingers. Place dried botanicals around the rim; glue them in place when you have a pleasing arrangement. Fill the basket halfway with crumpled tissue paper; cover the paper with moss. Fill the balance of the basket with dried rose petals or lavender blossoms and sprinkle with a few drops of essential oil.

CULINARY GARLAND

EDIBLE ART is a delectable way to enjoy garden favorites all year round. An earthy wreath, swag, or garland can be made with any combination of fragrant flavorful, air-dried herbs. It lends a rustic air and aromatic accent to the home—and keeps favorite herbs close at hand for everyday cooking. Just snip and toss as needed.

Make a wreath to suit your culinary fancy. If Italian fare is your preference then a garland of basil, parsley, oregano, and rosemary will spice up your home and your recipes. A gourmet who favors French cuisine might opt for a Provençal-inspired wreath of thyme, sage, dill, and lavender. And no Southwestern chef worth her salt would be without a *ristra*—a braid of the dried fiery red peppers used to ignite dips and chili dishes. An edible wreath is also a perfect gift. The next time you're invited to a dinner party, nourish your friends as well as your friendship with a garland of herbs from your garden.

To create my garland, I made a base by twisting sturdy jute twine and grapevines together. Then I made small bundles of herbs, tied them with raffia, and fastened them to the base with additional twine. The ends are embellished with cinnamon sticks.

FLAVORED VINEGAR

AKING FLAVORED vinegar is like making matches: the flavors must marry well for true happiness. Pair flowers, fruit, or delicate herbs with a light vinegar such as white wine, champagne, rice, or cider. Robust herbs and spices like garlic, sage, rosemary, oregano, chili peppers, and peppercorns need substantive mates such as balsamic, red wine, or sherry vinegar. Choose fruit, herbs, and flowers that are free of blemishes, mold or fungus, pesticides or herbicides, and insects.

Due to a chemical interaction, vinegar should not come into contact with metal; use glass containers when making vinegar. Sterilize new corks in boiling water. Do not reuse corks.

Fruit vinegar

1/2 lb. fresh fruit, mashed (berries, cherries, apricots, plums, or pears)

2 1/2 cups white, rice, or champagne vinegar

Sugar or honey, to taste

Combine fruit and vinegar in a sterilized glass jar. Cover and refrigerate to steep. Stir frequently. Check the flavor after 1 week. (It may take a month to attain the flavor you want.) Strain the vinegar through a coffee filter or cheesecloth. Discard the fruit. Place the vinegar in a saucepan, add sugar or honey to taste. Simmer over low heat for about 5 minutes. Let vinegar cool. Transfer to sterilized jars, add a few pieces of whole fruit if desired. Seal and date the jar; refrigerate for up to one year.

Herbal or floral vinegar

1 cup (28g) firmly packed fresh herbs or petals of edible flowers
(or 1/3 cup/9g, if dried)

Herbs: basil, oregano, rosemary or thyme

Flowers: calendula, lavender, nasturtium, rose or violet

2 cups (470ml) vinegar

Gently rinse herbs or flowers, pat dry on paper towels. Place ingredients in a sterilized glass container. Cover with a plastic-lined lid and refrigerate for 2 weeks. Turn and shake the bottle gently every day. When you are satisfied with the flavor, strain the vinegar through a coffee filter or cheesecloth. Discard the herbs and decant the liquid into a sterilized decorative bottle. Add a sprig or two of fresh herbs for garnish. Seal and date the jar; refrigerate for up to one year.

DELECTABLE SIDE DISHES

THE SCENT and flavors of the earth have great emotional pull on us all. I cannot taste wild mushrooms without thinking of invigorating treks through the autumn woods, the air redolent with the rich scents of soil and fallen leaves. I leave the picking to experts, however, to be safe, and always buy my wild or cultivated mushrooms from a reputable provider.

The steam-borne scent of saffron always takes me back to my mother's kitchen where Risotto alla Milanese (rice with saffron) was a staple dish. Risotto can be augmented with vegetables—zucchini, asparagus, or peas are popular additions—for variety or added nutrition.

Saffron, the stigmas of the flowers of *Crocus sativus*, is native to Asia. It has been known since ancient times and is a traditional flavoring of many European dishes. (This crocus can be grown in certain North American climates, but before you decide to grow your own saffron, remember that it takes approximately 3500 flowers to yield 1 ounce of the spice!)

Risotto alla Milanese

1/2 cup (125g) butter

1 tablespoon (15ml) olive oil

1 large onion, chopped fine

1 pound (450g) Arborio rice

1/2 cup (120ml) dry white wine

7 cups (1.6l) heated chicken stock or
low salt chicken broth

1 generous pinch of powdered saffron, dissolved
in 1/4 cup (60ml) heated stock

1 cup (135g) freshly grated Parmesan cheese

freshly ground black pepper

In a large, heavy saucepan, melt butter over medium heat. Add olive oil and onions, sauté until onions are translucent. Add rice, stir for 2 minutes. Add white wine, stir until it evaporates. Add 1/2 cup (120ml) of the heated stock; stir until absorbed. Continue adding stock, 1/2 cup (120ml) at a time and stirring until absorbed, until rice is tender and creamy (about 30 minutes). Stir in dissolved saffron. Add parmesan cheese and freshly ground black pepper to taste. Serves 6 as an entree, 8 as a side dish.

Wild Mushroom Pie

1/4 cup (60g) butter

1 tablespoon (15ml) olive oil

8 shallots, minced

3 pounds (1.4kg) fresh mixed wild mushrooms
(portobello, shiitake, cremini),
stems removed, wiped clean
and cut into large dice

Salt and pepper to taste

1/2 cup (120ml) dry sherry

1/2 cup (120ml) whipping cream

2 egg yolks, beaten lightly

9" prepared deep dish pie crust

Preheat oven to 375°F (191°C). Heat butter and olive oil in a large skillet over medium heat. Add shallots and sauté until soft. Add mushrooms and stir until they are browned, softened, and all the moisture is evaporated. Add sherry slowly; stir until absorbed. Add salt and pepper. Remove from heat and add cream a little at a time—just enough to moisten mushrooms. Cool to room temperature. Fold egg yolks into mushroom mixture. Pour mixture into pie crust. Bake for 50 to 60 minutes. Serves 6 as an entree, 8 as a side dish.

"But winter has yet brighter scenes, he boasts splendors beyond what gorgeous summer knows."

—WILLIAM CULLEN BRYANT

WINTER

WINTER RHAPSODY

 UTSIDE, THE New England landscape slumbers serenely under a blanket of snow. As I wander across our wintry garden in the early morning hours, there is a sense of solitude and tranquillity which is interrupted only by the occasional chirping of a few hardy birds.

There is a subtle beauty to a winter garden. It is a time when the architecture of the garden, its bones, are most noticeable. The bare branches of our century-old hickory glisten with icicles. The tree limbs' intricate shapes frame plumes of tall grasses swaying in the wind. Most of my perennials have long since retreated, but the stalwart blossoms of my sedum and hydrangeas remain, catching snowflakes as they swirl from the blustery sky. Our towering pines, the anchors of our garden, cast long shadows on the snow while underneath the miracle of nature lies waiting to stir again. It is a restorative time for garden and gardener alike.

When the flurry of holiday activities subsides and the new year begins, I curl up by a warm fire with stacks and stacks of seed and garden catalogs. With my red pen in hand, I eagerly circle my "must-haves." Each year I am determined to exert restraint when placing my seed order, but I always find myself marking far more than I can reasonably sow. How could I resist all the tantalizing descriptions of flavorful vegetables, vibrant flowers, and fruitful vines? While I remain rapt in the dream, my order grows and grows.

In late winter as the days begin to almost imperceptibly lengthen, my dormant winter garden starts to awaken, stretch, and yawn. The bright yellow buds of my witch hazel are swollen, any moment now they will burst open with a welcome shower of vivid color and refreshing scent. Drifts of snowdrops have begun to poke their dainty, indomitable heads up through the frozen ground. But here, in the mailbox at the end of my walk, is the surest sign of spring—my seeds have arrived!

"Anyone who thinks that gardening begins in the spring and ends in the fall is missing the best part of the year. For gardening begins in January, it begins with the dream."

—JOSEPHINE NUESE

A Winter Outing

My collection of Christmas ornaments grows bigger each year, and my annual search for the perfect tree upon which to display these sentimental treasures is launched right after Thanksgiving with a trip to a nearby Christmas tree farm.

An expedition to a tree farm to cut your own tree is a wonderful family tradition that gives you an opportunity to select from a wide range of truly fresh trees. Experiencing the woods in winter is exhilarating, but as long as your loved ones are with you, it doesn't matter where you find your tree—even the most urban corner lot will sing out Noel.

When we lived in New York City, I was always thrilled to see the vacant lots being transformed into miniature Christmas tree forests. Even though I was in the heart of Manhattan with the subway rumbling below my feet, the sight and scent of these majestic trees strung with twinkling lights made my heart soar with the joy of the season.

THINGS TO DO

Early

- Mulch garden beds after ground freezes.
- Collect fallen boughs, branches, and pine cones to use for holiday decorating.
- Check Christmas tree and poinsettias daily and water as needed to make sure they don't dry out.
- Decorate window boxes with holiday greenery and berries from the garden.
- Order seed catalogs.
- Write a Christmas wish list of garden goodies for yourself and friends.

Middle

- Use boughs from discarded Christmas trees as mulch over low-growing perennials.
- Check winter protection; secure and replace windbreaks around shrubs.
- Remove heavy snow from shrubs and evergreens to prevent branches from breaking.

*"If you truly love nature,
you will find beauty everywhere."*

—Vincent van Gogh

❧ Order seeds from catalogs for indoor sowing.

❧ Examine stored tubers and bulbs for excess moisture and rotting. Repack or change storage area as needed.

❧ Hard-prune any wisteria vines.

Late

❧ Prune trees, especially fruit trees, before they start spring growth.

❧ Remove dead and damaged branches from trees and shrubs.

❧ Reapply antidesiccant spray on evergreens, holly, and rhododendrons when temperature is above 40°F (15°C).

❧ Gently press any frost-heaved perennials back into soil.

❧ Start sowing seeds for herbs and hardy annuals indoors.

Ongoing

❧ Inspect houseplants for insects and diseases. Treat as needed.

❧ Keep bird feeders well stocked, replenish suet frequently, and provide a constant supply of fresh warm water.

❧ Clean and sharpen garden tools.

❧ Repair and paint garden furniture.

❧ Walk through the garden to decide what improvements or additions you would like to make.

❧ Plan and sketch ideas for your dream garden.

SPINACH

SWEET PEAS

FORGET-ME-NOT

BURT'S SEED FOR QUALITY

HYACINTH BEAN

No.616

DELPHINIUM

No.988

THE GARDEN HABITAT

HEN MY sister, Carolyn, bought her new home, she was told that deer lived in the nearby woods. She had imagined that occasionally she would see a single sweet doe gently nibbling on a rose. But she soon learned that where there is one deer, there are hordes of deer whose relentless hunger leads them to plunder the bountiful gardens thoughtfully provided by innocent homeowners.

Tulips and azaleas were spring's *plats du jour*. In summer, they dined on daylilies and sunflowers. The evergreens that surround the property were the fall and winter buffet.

There was no simple solution to her dilemma. Neither erecting a high fence around the property nor protecting prized greenery with wire cages was practical. Other deterrents—such as spraying with voodoo potions or hanging soap bars or string bags filled with human hair on branches—failed on practical and esthetic fronts.

We decided the only way to resolve this issue was to plant less-toothsome varieties. With the fervor of zealots, we researched botanicals that are unappetizing to deer. Deer are fickle eaters—their tastes change from place to place and season to season—so there is no such thing as a totally deer-resistant garden. In general, however, deer dislike fuzzy foliage and pungent aromas, so Carolyn's beds include lots of lamb's ears, black-eyed Susans, and globe thistles as well as mints, chives, ornamental onions and garlic, and herbs such as lavender and rosemary, dill, thyme, and yarrow. Deer also eschew many of the perennials favored for cottage-style gardening including foxglove, snapdragon, monkshood, and poppies. The list of evergreens is rather meager but spruce, juniper, boxwood, and Japanese andromeda can replace the more delectable ones.

In this ever-changing environment, it is possible to create a vibrant garden and still live in harmony with God's other creatures.

*"And Winter
slumbering in the open air
Wears on his smiling face
a dream of Spring!"*
—SAMUEL TAYLOR
COLERIDGE

December

THE HOLLY

OR CENTURIES, the winter solstice was celebrated with joy and merrymaking. The people knew that this day with the longest night was the turning point of the natural year: the days would begin to lengthen and the cold winter would gradually give way to the budding miracle of spring. At this moment, when most of the countryside lay barren, the gleaming green leaves and brilliant red berries of holly became a symbol of life's renewal and of man's universal hope for the future.

Early cultures believed that holly had the sun's particular blessing. How else could it retain its glossy deep green foliage and sparkling red berries throughout the harsh winter? Some also thought that holly possessed mystical powers, that its bright berries would ward off evil and its branches would protect a house from witches and demons. Others imagined that the plant itself was the home of elves and jovial gnomes so in winter they cut the boughs and brought them indoors to shelter the playful spirits from the inhospitable elements.

Today these beliefs have largely been abandoned, but holly still evokes a magical feeling at Yuletide and inspires faith in the ever-renewing cycle of seasons. In that spirit, I planted our first English holly *(Ilex aquifolium)* and dreamed of decking my halls with homegrown branches alight with crimson berries. But our beautiful tree produced nary a one. A little research yielded the answer. Hollies are dioecious—that is, they have male and female flowers on sep-

"Blessed is the season which engages the whole world in a conspiracy of love."

—HAMILTON W. MOBIE

arate plants—our female holly needed a mate to bear fruit. With the addition of a male tree and the industrious attention of bees and other fliers to pollinate the flowers in late spring and early summer, we now enjoy berry-laden branches.

Our holly trees grace our garden year-round, but it is during the holiday season, when their verdant boughs suggest hope for a bright new year for all, that we remember the traditions established by our early ancestors and truly cherish their beauty. And maybe on some magical moonlit night, I will catch a glimpse of gossamer pixies frolicking among the branches.

Planting Tips

The holly genus, Ilex, comprises more than 400 species; some varieties are evergreen, some deciduous. The best times for planting are early spring and early fall.

Prefers slightly acidic soil. Evergreen varieties prefer well-drained soil, deciduous hollies will also thrive in moist sites.

Deciduous hollies prefer sun in order to fruit well; other varieties tolerate light shade.

Dig the holes only as deep as the root balls. Plant at least two holly trees, one male and one female, to ensure fruiting. (One male plant can fertilize 12 females in a 100-foot/30-meter radius.)

Fertilize sparingly.

GARDENER'S CHRISTMAS TREE

OMETIMES THE sweetest decorations are the most natural—and certainly those that are lovingly made by hand are among the most cherished. Creating natural ornaments adds another dimension to the spirit of the season by reminding us of the Earth's fundamental bounty.

Our Christmas tree is in full bloom with preserved garden flowers, seasonal fruits, and gilded whimsies. Rosebud swags gaily wrap the tree like a flourish of ribbon. Fresh star fruit and dried orange slices catch the glow of tiny, starry lights and shine like stained glass. Gilded globe artichokes, pomegranates, and curly willow add a mellow note of gold, as do the tiny painted baskets brimming with fresh cranberries. Like snowflakes caught in midair, dried hydrangea and Queen

Anne's lace nestle snugly among the branches. Delicate bundles of dried feverfew, goldenrod, yarrow, and lady's mantle hang from brightly colored satin ribbons.

The serene center of the holiday flurry, an evergreen's woodland beauty is an enduring symbol of family traditions, of friendships old and new, and of the eternal magic of Christmas.

Cloaked in moss, star anise, and raffia, or studded with miniature rosebuds, humble Styrofoam balls become treasured heirloom ornaments.

"Whatever else may be lost among the years,
Let us keep Christmas still a shining thing."

—GRACE N. CROWELL

WELCOME GARLAND

RESSING THE house indoors and out for the holidays imparts the feeling that great care and love went into sharing the beauty of the season with others. The spirit of generosity that characterizes the holiday season starts with the front door where an inviting entryway welcomes guests to your home even before they cross the threshold.

Nothing quite conveys the spirit of the Yuletide season as much as an artfully embellished wreath hanging in a window or adorning a door. Echoing the natural theme of the wreath, the door is festooned with a glorious garland fashioned from purchased roping and gilded seasonal fruit—a traditional symbol of hospitality. Window boxes, urns, and planters overflowing with festive bouquets of evergreens complete the setting, sending the message of peace and good will.

Materials

- Evergreen roping
- Evergreen wreath
- Assorted embellishments: dried flowers and fresh fruit, such as cockscomb, pepperberries, kumquats, pine cones, pears, lemons, limes, pomegranates
- Floral picks, as needed
- Florist's wire, as needed
- Ribbon, as needed

Purchase wreath and roping from a garden center, craft shop, or Christmas tree vendor. (I chose a boxwood wreath and roping of laurel, cedar, and white pine.) To secure light fruit, bend a length of wire in half and push it through one piece, twist the ends together close to the fruit to prevent it from slipping off, then twist the wire around the wreath or garland. Pierce heavier fruit with a floral pick, then secure the pick to the base with florist's wire. (Replace fruit when no longer fresh.) Weave a length of ribbon through the greenery to complete the design.

"The hall
was dressed with
holly green;
forth to the wood
did merry men go
to gather in
the mistletoe."
—SIR WALTER SCOTT

FESTIVE SWAG

ECKING THE halls, staircases, mantels, and doors with swags of decorated greenery adds flourishes of grandeur to the holiday season. Nothing dresses up the house with Christmas warmth and cheer more than fragrant garlands do.

The dramatic double-story window that dominates our living room is an ideal backdrop for an elegantly decorated garland. Ropings of princess pine, boxwood, and white pine are twisted together and wrapped with gold cording to create a lush swag with many different textures and subtle variations of shades. Once the garland is securely in place (picture hangers and wire serve well for this), garnishes of holly, cedar, pomegranates, pine cones, and fresh roses tucked into water vials are nestled throughout the roping to create a lavish tapestry that will delight family and friends.

Gilded papier-mâché cherubs soar above, anchoring the corners of the swag and heralding the good news of the season.

YULETIDE CENTERPIECE

CHRISTMAS IS one of the most inspiring times of the year for flower arranging. Scouting the garden for interesting greens is a wonderful way to bring the spirit of the outdoors into your own home and onto your holiday table. Nature provides the most extraordinary gifts in abundance—evergreens with different textures, colors, needles and leaves; clusters of rich, ripe scarlet berries, medleys of nuts, pine cones and grasses; sparse branches, twisted twigs and gnarled vines. The rich array of trimmings just outside our doors is the perfect complement to the flowers and fruit available at this time of year.

You can create a festive holiday arrangement guaranteed to put a sparkle in your guests' eyes. Whether you're planning a dramatic centerpiece in a footed glass compote for a formal sit-down dinner or a casual bouquet in a willow basket for a rustic buffet, the combination of seasonal greenery, flowers, fruits, and candles will bring a warm glow to any holiday setting.

Materials

- Decorative container
- Florist's foam
- Assorted seasonal greenery: pine sprays with cones or berries; broad- and small-leafed evergreens
- Berries: skimmia, winterberry, juniper blueberry, rose hips, hypericum, berried ivy
- Fresh flowers
- Candles (slow-burning, nondrip)

Soak florist's foam in water, place it in the container. (I chose an inexpensive plastic candelabrum, and spray-painted it gold.) Starting from center, push the stems of the greenery and flowers into the foam. Use an assortment of greens and flowers for a striking combination of colors and textures. Use odd numbers of each item included and let the arrangement fall naturally. To be certain that the final arrangement will be pleasing from all sides, keep turning the container as you work. Caution: Never leave candles burning unattended. Extinguish and replace candles when they have burned to within 3 inches (8cm) of the foliage.

MANTEL

THE LIVING room hearth is the heart of our home and the place where I most like to spend time during the holiday season. The sight of blazing Yule logs, the scent of balsam lingering in the air, an enticing pot of herbal tea and a sampling of Christmas goodies make this an inviting place to gather with friends and family.

The fireplace mantel is a natural focus for decorating. Boughs of pine, spruce, and cedar from the garden create a woodsy backdrop for sprigs of holly, colorful rose hips and pepperberries, skimmia, and ivy berries.

At Christmas we are inspired to bring out the best of our precious keepsakes. They hold the stories of people and places we cherish. The turn-of-the-century silver tankards I've nestled among the evergreens have been lovingly passed down from one generation to another and are a treasured remembrance of times past. In the place of honor, a beloved angel perches on the edge of the mantel, keeping silent watch over all, a symbol of the true spirit of the season.

ALL THAT GLITTERS

**HE HOLIDAY** season is a time to shine. Use your own Midas touch to devise glittering holiday decorations that sparkle with silver, shimmer in gold, and twinkle like stardust. With one swift stroke of the brush, glossy green magnolia leaves are metamorphosed into a rich burnished gold. Next a pale yellow quince disappears and, almost magically, a gilded Fabergé-inspired egg appears in its stead. Lightly sprayed hydrangeas become airy puffs of spun gold. Artichokes, pomegranates, pine cones, nuts, grasses, and wheat are all delightfully transformed when painted ever-so-lightly with glorious gold. And simple clay pots become Florentine works of art when sponged with silver or gold. Try forging your own unique creations. Whether you paint, spray, or sponge, your glittering greens will radiate holiday cheer.

Materials

🌿 Gold paint, liquid or spray

🌿 Assorted botanicals, containers, and ornaments

🌿 Natural sponges, old saucer or jar lid
(if sponge painting)

🌿 Brushes (if painting)

Spray painting Work in a well-ventilated area. Protect the surrounding work area with newspaper. Spray fruit lightly until covered. Set aside to dry. If you will be making many ornaments, wear a dust mask and rubber gloves.

Sponging Protect the work surface with newspaper. Fill an old saucer or jar lid with liquid paint. Dip the sponge in the paint, dab it on the newspaper to remove any excess, then pat the item with the sponge. Set aside to dry.

Painting Protect the work surface with newspaper. Using a brush, work as for sponging.

Frosted Fruit & Flowers

4 pounds (2kg) assorted seasonal fruit

Edible flowers (see p. 77)

2/3 cup of meringue powder
mixed with 6 to 8 tablespoons of water

1 1/2 cups (300gm) extrafine sugar

Decorative flowers and holiday greens

Wash fruit and pat dry. Place a sheet of wax paper on a wire rack. Mix meringue powder with enough water to form a thin paste. Using a pastry brush, paint a thin layer of meringue over one piece of fruit. Working over a plate or tray, sprinkle sugar over fruit until all sides are coated. Shake gently to remove excess sugar. Place sugared fruit on paper-lined rack. Continue with remaining fruit and edible flowers. Set rack aside in a warm dry place for several hours until sugar hardens. Arrange in a decorative container. Add fresh flowers and greens for decoration, if desired.

VISIONS OF SUGARPLUMS

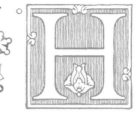

OLIDAY FESTIVITIES are made all the sweeter with an elegant arrangement of sugar-frosted fruit and flowers. This combination of grapes, apples, pears, and citrus with roses and lilies was inspired by the still life paintings of 17th-century Dutch masters.

The impressive results come from very simple means. The fruit and flowers are coated with moistened meringue powder (available at stores that sell fine cake-decorating supplies) and sprinkled with white or colored sugar. Arrange the frosted fruit on a pedestal plate or on decorative plates on a tiered stand. Tuck fresh flowers and greens into water vials and use them to enhance the display—and to discourage nibbling inedible elements. If family and friends can resist it, this festive arrangement will serve as a feast for the eyes for several days.

Materials

- Balsam fir clippings
- Sprigs of dried rosemary, dill, marjoram, lavender
- Juniper twigs with berries
- Cinnamon sticks
- Raffia or jute

Assemble a mixed bundle of fragrant sprigs and tie it with jute or raffia. Piled in a basket, the raffia-tied kindling bundles make charming hearth decorations. (Use a fire screen to protect the kindling from flying sparks.)

SCENTED KINDLING

EVEN WITH my eyes closed, I know Christmas is coming. The entire house is filled with the unmistakable scents of the Yuletide season. The balsam and spruce boughs in the living room exude the rich woodsy aroma of a Christmas tree forest. Bowls of pine cones rolled in spices lend a warm and folksy fragrance to the kitchen. But of all these enticing aromas, none is more inviting than that of logs crackling in the fireplace. Enhance this delicious olfactory experience by making small bundles of fragrant herbs to add to the fire. The evocative scent will draw friends and family to the hearth as soon as they step through the front door.

TOPIARY

HE ART OF shaping topiaries was first perfected by the Romans. They also coined a word—*topiarius*—to describe these ornamental gardens. By the end of the 17th century, William of Orange had elevated the training of ornamental plants to high art. The European aristocracy soon followed suit and created formal gardens composed of individual plants sculpted into complex imaginative shapes. These ornate topiaries required the diligent labor of many hands to pinch, clip, and prune the foliage to keep it at its peak.

In the 19th century the Victorian passion for ornament and delight in gardening converged in topiary. Victorians enthusiastically adorned

There are several kinds of topiaries: portable forms (such as the swan), standards, and sculpted shrubs. Portable forms function as the container for the plant. Plants that root easily such as ivy and creeping fig are the best choice for these forms. Standard topiaries are usually fashioned from potted plants such as lavender, rosemary, and myrtle that have been guided around wire frames or pruned at intervals to create desired shapes. Spirals, spheres, and ball-over-ball are popular shapes. Privet, yew, and boxwood are good choices for sculpting.

both their parlors and vast conservatories with endless versions of topiaries. Their gardens were most often showcases for tree and shrub topiaries of enormous proportions. In recent times, this fanciful garden art has broadened its appeal. No longer strictly for the estates of the wealthy, topiaries now flourish happily near cottages as well as castles.

I am enchanted with my topiaries. They are living architectural forms that add charm and whimsy to my home and garden. They seem to take on magical lives of their own. Each topiary can be as simple or elaborate as desired and as individual as the gardener herself. Trimming, training, and maintaining a topiary takes patience, but the results are well worth the time and effort.

BIRD TREAT TREE

AFTER THE celebration of Epiphany on January 6th, our Christmas tree is retired from its role of inspiring good cheer inside the house and goes outdoors to be enjoyed by our native birds. Redecorating the Christmas tree with a buffet of tasty treats is as much fun as the first holiday decorating, and a creative way to bring the festivities outdoors.

Even the most finicky feathered diva is guaranteed to find something irresistible on a tree festooned with clusters of wheat, milo, and millet; bagel halves slathered with peanut butter and sprinkled with birdseed; orange and grapefruit halves filled with birdseed, peanuts, and black-oil sunflower seeds; and pine cones coated with peanut butter and rolled in birdseed. Popcorn and cranberry garlands are pretty as well as tasty, as are tiny lady apples, rose hips, bundles of corn and ribbon-tied nosegays of dried sunflowers, black-eyed Susans, and purple coneflowers.

To supplement your handmade edible decorations, buy an assortment of ready-made birdseed ornaments at your local garden center. They come in a variety of charming shapes—moons, stars, bells, hearts. After the birds have plucked them clean, these wooden cutouts can be reused—you only need to recoat them with peanut butter and birdseed.

Providing a treat-laden tree to feed local birds is a rewarding way to prolong the generosity of the season.

"A garden without birds is like a garden without flowers."

—CANON HENRY ELLACOMBE

BIRDHOUSES

 INTER IS an ideal time to build a new birdhouse. It can be as simple or elaborate as you like, but a few features are universally desirable. Make the entrance hole the right size for the species you wish to attract. Bore drainage holes to prevent flooding, and ventilation holes for air and light. Provide a rough surface below the entrance, both inside and out, for easy access. After that, you should research the particular needs of the birds you prefer and include those features.

To discourage predators, mount the house on top of a pole and add a protective collar below it. If you hang the house on a tree limb, choose one at least six feet off the ground. Birds enjoy sunshine, so avoid giving the entrance a northern exposure. A removable panel makes cleaning easier.

Providing the right birdhouse will increase the likelihood of attracting more birds to your garden. You will have the pleasure of viewing these winsome creatures closeup, and they will make your gardening days more enjoyable with their sweet songs and their voracious appetites for insects.

"Ye gentle birds, the world's fair ornament, And heaven's glory."
—EDMUND SPENSER

BLOOMING LAMP SHADE

OUTSIDE MY bedroom window the world is blanketed with snow. Icicles dangle like crystal prisms from the eaves and frost forms a misty coating on the windowpanes. Now is the perfect time to create springtime magic indoors. Casting about for a project, I decide that the gentle radiance of a "blooming" lamp shade would be just the thing to lend a touch of romance to the boudoir.

Crowned with clusters of lush, blushing cottage roses, this simple little lamp is transformed from humble to *haute couture*. And, for a whimsical moment, I'm tempted to wear it on my head. But I resist the urge, sprinkle a few drops of rose-scented essential oil over the flowers and place the lamp on the night table. There the gentle warmth of the low-wattage bulb will coax the perfume into the air and sweeten dreams with the intoxicating fragrance of an old-fashioned rose garden on a late summer's afternoon.

Materials

- Lamp shade and base
- Freeze-dried roses
- Hot-glue gun and glue sticks, as needed
- Essential oil
- Low-wattage bulb

Working from the bottom up, dab hot glue on the shade, then gently press a flower in place. Add flowers in rows around the shade until it is completely covered. Freeze-dried flowers are a little brittle, handle them carefully. Sprinkle a few drops of essential oil over the completed shade. Use only low-wattage bulbs; excessive heat could damage the shade. No need to water —this bouquet will bloom eternally.

*"The red rose whispers of passion,
And the white rose breathes of love."*
—JOHN BOYLE O'REILLY

PARTY HORS D'OEUVRES

THERE'S NO better way to ring in the New Year than by inviting friends and family to share in the celebration. Beautifully presented finger food complements both formal and casual affairs. And because hors d'oeuvres can be enjoyed standing up, they help generate a more sociable ambiance. Sharing these tasty morsels encourages easy conversation. Whether a party is for 4 or 40, these easy recipes are guaranteed to tempt your guests.

Sun-dried Tomato & Olive Tapenade

8-ounce (227g) jar oil-packed sun-dried tomatoes (do not drain)

3 medium-size garlic cloves, peeled

1 tablespoon finely chopped parsley

1/2 cup (62g) chopped pitted Kalamata olives

2 teaspoons capers

12-ounce (340g) goat cheese log

French baguette bread, cut into thin slices and toasted

1 head Belgian endive

Combine sun-dried tomatoes (with oil) and garlic in food processor. Transfer mixture to bowl and mix in parsley, olives, and capers. Wash endive and separate leaves. Spoon tapenade over goat cheese and serve with toasted bread rounds and endive leaves. Serve at room temperature. Yield: approximately 1 1/2 cup (360ml).

"To invite a person into your house is to take charge of his happiness for as long as he is under your roof."

—ANTHELME BRILLAT-SAVARIN

Artichoke Dip

1 medium-size fresh artichoke

1 can (14 oz/397g) artichoke hearts in water

1/4 cup (60ml) mayonnaise, full- or low-fat

1/2 cup (120ml) dairy sour cream, full- or low-fat

1 teaspoon finely chopped basil

1/2 cup (62g) shredded cheese (Edam, Gouda, or Parmesan)

Assorted dipping vegetables: red peppers, baby carrots, cherry tomatoes, pea pods, broccoli and cauliflower florets

Blanch fresh artichoke, remove center leaves, choke, and heart. Drain canned artichoke hearts and chop coarsely. In a food processor, combine artichoke hearts, mayonnaise, sour cream, basil, and cheese; blend until smooth. To serve, spread outer leaves of blanched artichoke, spoon dip into center of the artichoke. Place on a tray and surround with dipping vegetables. Yield: approximately 1 1/2 cups (360ml)

BOTANICAL BATH OIL

THE SHEER enjoyment of luxuriating in a bath filled with delicate botanical essences has a restorative effect on the mind, body, and soul. Each botanical combination can be blended to be relaxing or invigorating, as you wish. The soothing scents of jasmine, lavender, rose, and ylang-ylang are among my favorites. Stimulating aromas include eucalyptus, rosemary, peppermint, lemon, grapefruit, and juniper. Citrus and mint oils are so stimulating, in fact, that they must be used with extreme moderation—2 to 3 drops of oil to a tub full of water. Citrus oils may also increase your skin's sensitivity to the sun. (Avoid exposure for up to six hours after use.)

Pampering yourself with an aromatic bath is a magical experience that delights the senses, revives the body, and energizes the spirit.

Fill a decorative bottle with a carrier oil such as jojoba or sweet almond oil. Keep it pure and use it as the base to make blended bath oils on the spur of the moment to suit particular moods, whims, or needs.

Preparation

2 cups (480ml) cold-pressed carrier oil: sweet almond, jojoba, apricot kernel, or grapeseed oil

Assorted botanicals (for decoration, if desired)

Soothing blend of essential oils:
1/4 teaspoon each lavender, ylang-ylang, and rose

Stimulating blend of essential oils:
1/4 teaspoon each eucalyptus and rosemary

Mix carrier oil and essential oils in a clean, stoppered glass bottle. Rinse botanicals and pat dry. Add to bottle, cover, and shake well. Use 1 or 2 teaspoons of oil in a warm bath (add while water is running). Experiment with your favorite scents, but try to keep the quantities in the same ratio as here. Store in a cool, dark place. Caution: For external use only. Keep out of the reach of children. Test before using; any oil may provoke an allergic reaction. Always dilute essential oils before using. Avoid use near or around eyes. If pregnant, do not use. People with health concerns should consult a doctor or certified aromatherapist before using.

THE SNOWDROP

 HILE MOST of the garden slumbers in deep hibernation, throngs of intrepid snowdrops burst onto the garden scene and awaken the spirit of hope and promise. Few flowers are as gratifying as these dainty, indomitable blooms, and my admiration for them is immense. I am so enchanted by them that I dig up several clumps to put in pots indoors where their snowy white petals and honey-scented nectar can be enjoyed closeup. The shimmering white teardrop-shaped flowers will continue in full bloom for up to three weeks. Then, when they are through blooming, I replant them in the garden to restore their vigor and ensure that their beauty can be admired throughout the many seasons to come.

Outdoors in the garden these seemingly fragile flowers continue to push up through the snow and ice, announcing the end of winter and the fast-approaching spring. This resilient vitality inspired the Victorians to designate the snowdrop as the symbol of hope in their language of flowers.

Watching these early risers sway to the rhythm of the wailing winter winds I can't help but think of the lines in Percy Bysshe Shelley's *Ode to the West Wind*— "The trumpet of a prophecy! O wind, / If Winter comes, can Spring be far behind?" Each year in my garden their doughty presence signifies the renewal of nature's unending cycle of life.

"Blessings upon thee, gentle bud of hope!"

—HARTLEY COLERIDGE

SEEDS

EBRUARY IS spelled "c-a-t-a-l-o-g-s" in the gardener's dictionary. But whether you order something exotic from a catalog or pick up old favorites at the store, start your seeds in timely manner. To ensure having garden-ready seedlings when your garden is ready, find out the approximate date of the last frost in your area, count back 6 to 8 weeks (include the germination period), and sow the seeds then.

To start seeds indoors, gather an assortment of containers. Peat pots or flats are excellent—pot and all can be planted directly into the garden. Clean empty milk cartons, cottage cheese or yogurt containers, and lidded plastic take-out containers also work well. (Punch holes in the bottom for drainage.)

Use a commercial seed-starting mix. Moisten it with warm water and leave it overnight. Then fill the containers to within one-half inch (1cm) of the top, add the seeds, and cover, or not, as described on the package. Label the containers with indelible ink and cover them with clear plastic wrap propped up with toothpicks. Water carefully to avoid disturbing the seeds.

Seeds need warmth to germinate. Set the trays on top of the refrigerator or on a horticultural heat mat. After they sprout, remove the cover and move them to a sunny window or under fluorescent light. Keep the soil moist and apply a liquid fertilizer diluted to half strength once a week.

RUSTIC ARCHWAY

STEPPING through my rustic archway, I feel a bit like Dorothy stepping into the colorful land of Oz. Even though my brick "road" is red, it guides my feet on an enchanting journey from the house to the garden. The arch is not just an entrance, it is also a frame for the changing tableaux of the garden, and an ornament that celebrates the seasons' changing cycles of beauty.

My husband and I wanted a "back-to-nature" style so we used fallen tree limbs and saplings as a base. These were set in holes 10 to 12 inches (25 to 30cm) deep and anchored with compacted soil. Then we simply layered branches around the limbs, securing them with galvanized wire. Let the style of your home and the materials native to your area inspire you. A natural structure in the garden supplies dimension, height, visual impact—and a hint of intrigue.

GARDEN WHIMSIES

WHEN I WAS growing up, a garden was meant for growing tomatoes, peppers, and a few roses. Today my gardening enthusiasms embrace not only beautiful flowers and tasty vegetables, but also planting my outdoor space with decorative sculpture and ornaments. I think of my garden as an extension of my home. Just as each of my indoor rooms is furnished with a certain distinctive style, the same creative

expression is given to fashioning visually inviting outdoor rooms.

Artful embellishments will make your winter garden as captivating as your summer one—and treasure hunting for garden ornaments at flea markets, antique shows, and auctions is a welcome winter pastime. Whether old or new, formal or folksy, serious or playful, garden ornaments transform a workaday space into a unique and highly personal setting.

A cherub brings life to a quiet corner and a fountain graced with a flute player evokes music all year round. Smooth steppingstones form a garden path. A copper-and-brass sundial gleams brightly in the sun and softly when winter moonlight reflects off new-fallen snow. Salvaged finials, columns, and plaques add architectural interest and a touch of antiquity to the setting. A willow bench nestled under a shade tree promises a delightful spot for reading.

Whether you have acres, a slender backyard plot, or a small balcony above a cityscape, you can create your very own Shangri-la with an array of fanciful garden whimsies. Choose what you love and let your imagination take flight.

SWEETHEART WREATH

SENDING A message of affection and friendship to a loved one with the language of flowers is a special way to celebrate the spirit of Valentine's Day. This romantic holiday has always been a favorite of mine. I still hold dear a treasured cache of old-fashioned valentines and romantic mementos. The edges of the lacy antique doily hearts are yellow with age, but the warm sentiment of these keepsakes remains true.

Treat your sweetheart to a wreath adorned with clusters of blushing roses. Freeze-dried flowers and heart-shaped wreath bases are available at craft shops and garden centers. A few dabs of hot glue will secure the flowers. A flourish of ribbon completes the design. As a charming symbol of love and affection, your gift from the heart will be cherished by that someone special for many years to come.

"I love thee with the breath, Smiles, tears, of all my life!"

—ELIZABETH BARRETT BROWNING

> "What is more lovely than a flaming rose That blooms, more felt than seen, within the heart."
>
> –MALCOLM SCHLOSS

RED ROSE POMANDER

 ILL YOUR living room, bedroom, or entrance hall with the scent and beauty of year-round blooming roses. This decorative floral ball, abloom with dozens of sweet smelling miniature rose blossoms, is an evocative way to preserve the scent and sight of a summertime garden. As a handcrafted expression of cherished friendship, an old-fashioned rose pomander makes a memorable Valentine's Day gift.

Materials

- White glue
- 6-inch (15-cm) Styrofoam ball
- Sheet moss, as needed
- Decorative urn or clay pot (optional)
- Preserved miniature roses
- Hot-glue gun and glue sticks, as needed
- Rose-scented essential oil

Working in sections, cover ball with white glue and press sheet moss onto glue until entire surface is covered. Allow glue to set. Place ball in urn. Dab hot glue to bottom of one rose, press it into place on the moss (start from the top), and hold until glue sets. Work in rows around the ball and set the flowers as close together as possible. Handle the ball gently to avoid crushing the flowers. When done, sprinkle with rose-scented essential oil.

SWEET SURPRISES

ICH AND satisfying, chocolate makes even the most ordinary of occasions special. Luscious giant strawberries dipped in layers of chocolate are an enticing accompaniment to champagne and a perfect way to sweeten a romantic evening. Indulge with chocolate marble surprise—its crunchy texture and fanciful combinations make it enormous fun to eat. Whether opulently wrapped in layers of swirling tulle or simply served in a rustic basket, these seductive confections are a chocolate lover's dream.

Double-Dipped Strawberries

1 lb (455g) large long-stem strawberries

6 oz (170g) semisweet chocolate, chopped

4 oz (115g) white chocolate, chopped

Red sugar sprinkles or sparkling red sugar (optional)

Wash strawberries and pat dry; do not remove stems. Line a large cookie sheet with waxed paper. In the bottom of a double boiler, bring 2 cups (480ml) of water to simmering. Place dark chocolate in top of double boiler and set over simmering water. Stir gently until chocolate is completely melted. Remove top pot. Holding one strawberry by its stem, dip 2/3 of the berry into the melted chocolate. Let excess chocolate drip back into pot. Place berry on cookie sheet. Repeat with remaining berries. Place in refrigerator until chocolate is firm. Melt white chocolate. Take dipped strawberries from refrigerator and dip bottom portion in melted white chocolate. Sprinkle with red sugar, if desired. Return berries to refrigerator. Dipped strawberries can be kept in the refrigerator uncovered for several hours. Remove from refrigerator approximately 10 minutes before serving. Makes 12 to 15 dipped strawberries.

Chocolate Marble Surprise

6 oz (170g) semisweet chocolate, chopped

1 1/4 lb (624g) white chocolate, chopped

3/4 cup (85g) slivered almonds (toasted)

Red soft gel paste food coloring

To toast almonds, preheat oven to 350°F (177°C). Spread almonds on a cookie sheet. Place in oven for 10 minutes. Stir nuts a few times while cooking.

ๆ

Black & white chocolate swirl: Line a 13x9x5/8 cookie sheet with waxed paper. Place semisweet chocolate in a microwave-safe bowl. Microwave for 2 minutes; remove from oven and stir. If not fully melted, return to oven and heat as needed. Repeat with 8 oz/227g (about one third) of the white chocolate. Spread melted dark chocolate over half of the cookie sheet. Spread melted white chocolate next to it. Swirl chocolates together with a blunt knife. Sprinkle with half the toasted almonds. Refrigerate until firm (about one hour).

ๆ

Pink & white swirl: Melt the remaining white chocolate, then divide it in half. Stir enough food coloring into one half of the chocolate to tint it pink. Work as for black and white swirl. Yield: approximately 1 1/2 pounds (680g).

"To the attentive eye,
each moment of the year
has its own beauty,
and in the same field it beholds,
every hour, a picture which
was never seen before,
and which shall never
be seen again."

—RALPH WALDO
EMERSON

RESOURCES

FLOWERS, HERBS, & VEGETABLES
W. Atlee Burpee & Co.
300 Park Avenue
Warminster, PA 18974
800-888-1447

The Cook's Garden
P.O. Box 5010
Hodges, SC 29653-5010
800-457-9703

Gurney's
110 Capital Street
Yankton, SD 57079
605-665-1930

Halifax Seed Company Inc.
Box 8026, Station A
Halifax, NS
B3K 5L8
902-454-7456

Johnny's Selected Seeds
1 Foss Hill Road
Albion, ME 04910-9731
207-437-4301

Park Seed Company
1 Parkton Avenue
Greenwood, SC 29647-0001
800-845-3369

Richters Herbs
357 Highway 47
Goodwood, ON
L0C 1A0
905-640-6677

Shepherd's Garden Seeds
30 Irene Street
Torrington, CT 06790-6658
860-482-3638

Thompson & Morgan
P.O. Box 1308
Jackson, NJ 08527-0308
800-274-7333

HEIRLOOM PLANTS & SEEDS
The Antique Rose Emporium
9300 Lueckemeyer Road
Brenham, TX 77833
800-441-0002

Arena Rose Company
P.O. Box 3096
Paso Robles, CA 93447
805-227-4094

Seed Savers Exchange
3076 North Winn Road
Decorah, IA 52101
319-382-5990

Seeds of Diversity Canada
Box 36, Station Q
Toronto, ON
M4T 2L7

Select Seeds
180 Stickney Hill Road
Union, CT 06076
860-684-9310

BULBS, CORMS & RHIZOMES
Cruickshank's, Inc.
780 Birchmount Road, Unit 16
Scarborough, ON
M1K 5H4
800-665-5605

Daffodil Mart
30 Irene Street
Torrington, CT 06790-6658
800-255-2852

John Scheepers, Inc.
23 Tulip Drive
Bantam, CT 06750
860-567-0838

Van Bourgondien
245 Rt. 109
Babylon, NY 11702
800-622-9997

PERENNIALS & ROSES
Dominion Seed House
Box 2500
Georgetown, ON
L7G 5L6
905-873-3037

Jackson & Perkins
12 Rose Lane
Medford, OR 97501
800-292-4769

Spring Hill Nurseries
6523 North Galena Road
Peoria, IL 61632
800-582-8527

Wayside Gardens
1 Garden Lane
Hodges, SC 29695-0001
800-845-1124

White Flower Farm
P.O. Box 50
Litchfield, CT 06759-0050
800-503-9624

AROMATHERAPY & POTPOURRI SUPPLIES
Aphrodisia
264 Bleecker Street
New York, NY 10014
212-989-6440

Aroma Vera
5901 Rodeo Road
Los Angeles, CA 90016-4312
800-669-9514

Capriland's Herb Farm
534 Silver Street
Coventry, CT 06238
860-742-7244

The Essential Oil Company
1719 SE Umatilla
Portland, OR 97202
800-729-5912

The Herbal Touch
Box 300
30 Dover Street
Otterville, ON
N0J 1R0
519-879-6812

Oak Ridge Farms
P.O. Box 28
Basking Ridge, NJ 07920-0028
800-444-8843

San Francisco Herb Co.
250 14th Street
San Francisco, CA 94103
800-227-4530

Trouvez
2237 Chemin des Patriotes
Richelieu, QC
J3L 4A7
514-658-7311

PRESERVED FLOWERS & FOLIAGE
Flying B Bar Ranch
1100 McMullen Creek Road
Selma, OR 97538
888-729-0010

Lavender & Old Lace
P.O. Box 4983
Missoula, MT 59806
800-728-9244

Lilac Rose
1117 East Van Owen Avenue
Orange, CA 92867
800-530-1231

Strawflower Ridge
541 Darlings Island Road
Hampton, NB
E0G 1Z0
506-832-4827

TOPIARY FRAMES
Cliff Finch's Zoo
P.O. Box 54
Friant, CA 93626
209-822-2315

Mission Hills Nursery
1525 Fort Stockton Drive
San Diego, CA 92103
619-295-2808

HABITAT
Backyard Wildlife Habitat Program
National Wildlife Federation
8925 Leesburg Pike
Vienna, VA 22184-0001
800-822-9919

The Bug Store
113 West Argonne Street
St. Louis, MO 63122
800-455-2847

GARDEN ORNAMENTS & STRUCTURES
Florentine Craftsmen
46-24 28th Street
Long Island City, NY 11101
800-971-7600

Kenneth Lynch & Sons
84 Danbury Road
Wilton, CT 06897
203-762-8363

New England Garden Ornaments
P.O. Box 235
North Brookfield, MA 01535
508-867-4474

CREDITS

Illustrations

JEREMY DAWSON, calligraphy: 17, 59, 101, 143, and illustrations: 8-183
MICK ELLISON, decorative borders: 16-17, 58-59, 100-101, 142-143
JACQUES HNIZDOVSKY, woodcuts: 20 (bottom), 62 (bottom), 70-71(center), 84, 87 (right), 95 (bottom), 96, 109, 123 (right)

Acknowledgments

The author would also like to thank the following people and companies, all located in Connecticut:

ANTHROPOLOGIE, Westport
ANTIQUE AND ARTISAN CENTER, Stamford
BUNGALOW, Westport
CATHERINE SYLVIA REISS, INC., Darien
CRYSTAL GARDENS, Darien
GREENWICH ORCHIDS & FINE FLOWERS, Greenwich
HÔTEL (EUROPEAN HOTEL SILVER) Darien
LILLIAN AUGUST, Westport & Greenwich
MCARDLE-MACMILLEN GARDEN CENTER, Greenwich
PARC MONCEAU, Westport
SALVATORE AND GIACOMO GIGLIO, South Norwalk
REYNOLDS FARM NURSERIES, Norwalk

Special thanks to Tommy Simpson of Washington, Connecticut, for the use of his magnificently restored 1939 Ford pickup truck (photograph, page 19).

Photographs

ELEANOR THOMPSON: 8 (bottom), 9 (top, bottom)-11, 14 (top), 15-17, 19, 20, 26-34, 40, 42-46, 49 (upper), 51, 53-59, 61, 62, 71, 74-78, 81, 84-86, 88, 94, 96-101, 103 (top right), 104, 108, 109, 112-118, 120-128, 130, 132-141, 145, 146, 152-162, 164-172, 176, 177, 179-185

MAGGIE OSTER: 8 (top), 9 (middle), 12, 13, 14 (bottom), 24 (middle, left), 25, 36-39, 41, 48, 49 (bottom), 50, 52, 66-70, 72, 73, 80, 82, 83, 90, 91-93, 95, 103 (top left and bottom), 110, 111, 150, 151, 174, 175

MICHAEL MUFFOLETTO: 24 (top), 142, 143, 178 (top)

MELANIE HULSE: 178 (bottom)

Locations

We were fortunate in being able to photograph at several wonderful sites. The author thanks the following for their hospitality and generosity:

A & J'S OLD FASHIONED FARMSTAND, Westport, CT, 61
GANIM'S CHRISTMAS TREE FARM, Easton, CT, 145
HEATHER NETHERWOOD, Redding, CT, 14, 96, 113
HOLLANDIA NURSERY & GARDEN CENTER, Bethel, CT, 19
OUTHOUSE ORCHARDS, Croton Falls, NY, 103 (top right), 108, 109, 120-121(top)

INDEX

*Page numbers in **bold** type refer to text and photographs. **Bold italic** indicates photographs only.*

INDEX